Inspired Colors

Heather Eslinger

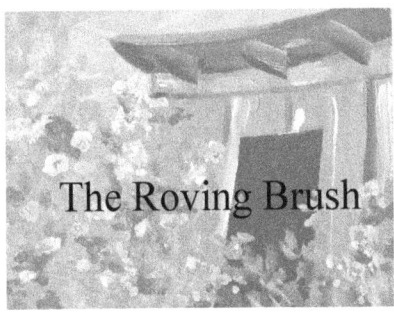

The Roving Brush

ISBN-13: 978-1983467509
ISBN-10: 1983467502

I dedicate this book of inspirational quotes
to my three sisters;
Rose, Heidi and Jewel.
You are strong, amazing women,
without you I would never have survived
the biggest obstacles of my life.
Thank you for your constant support
and for being my inspiration.

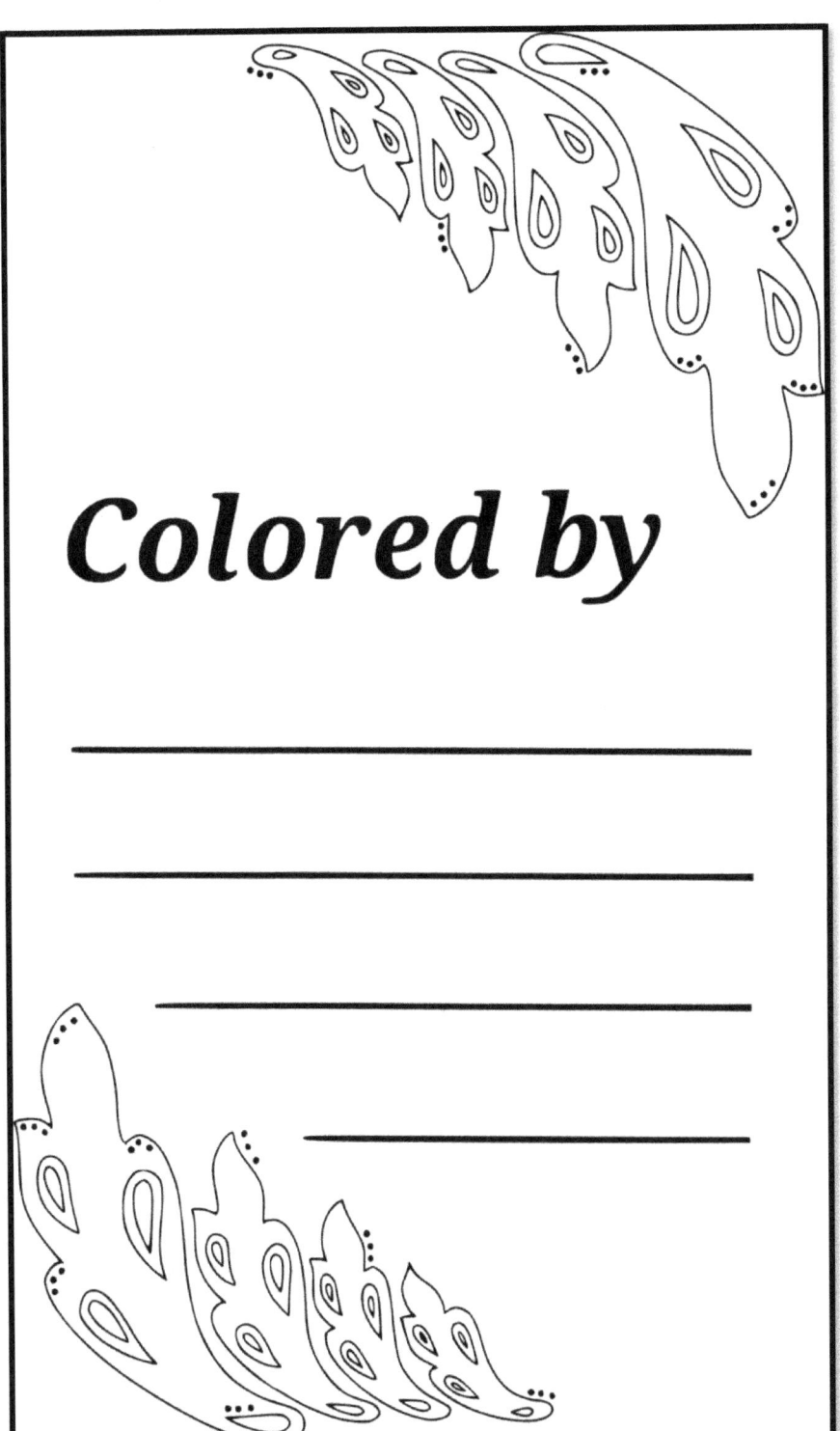

Colored by

_____

_____

_____

_____

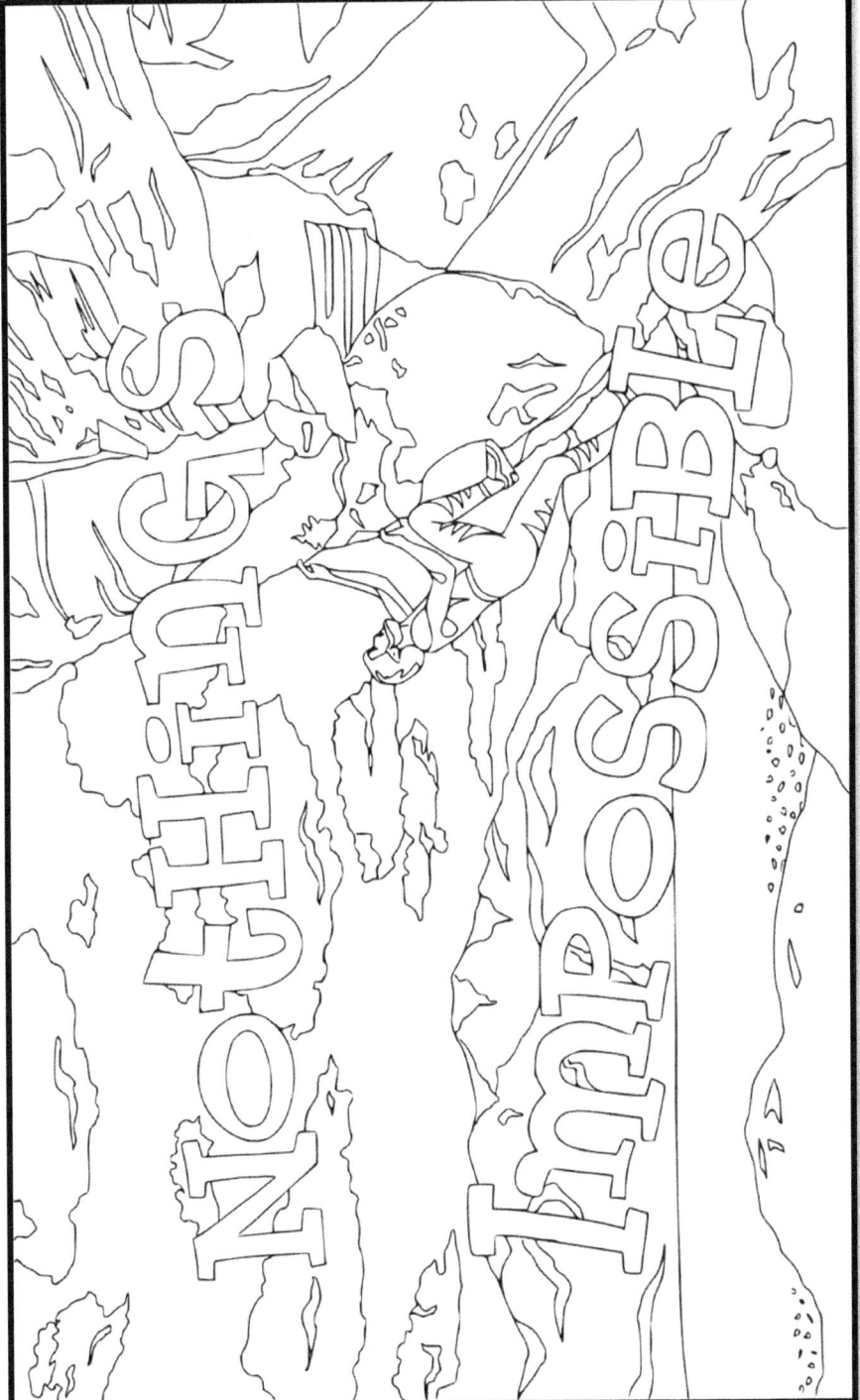

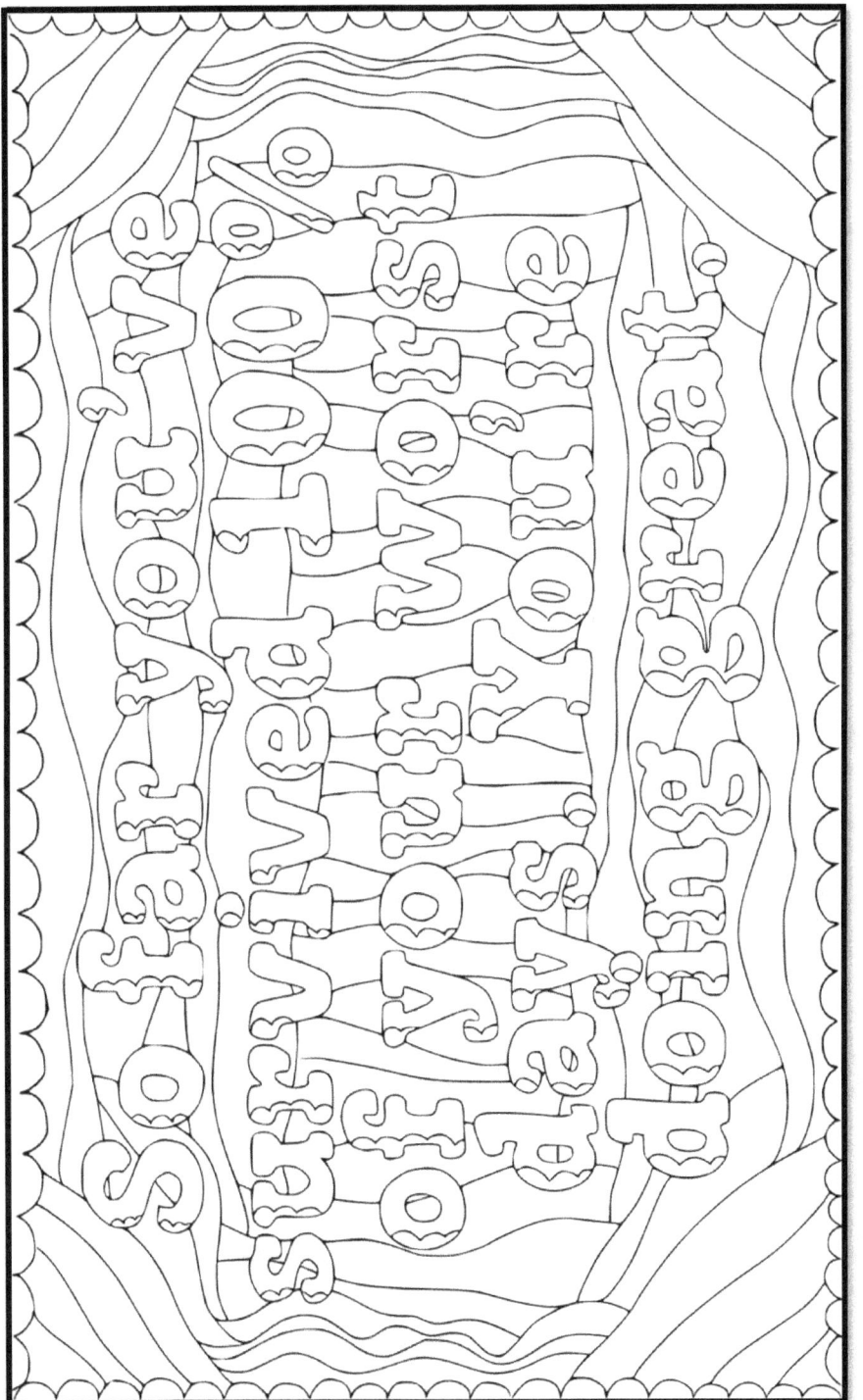

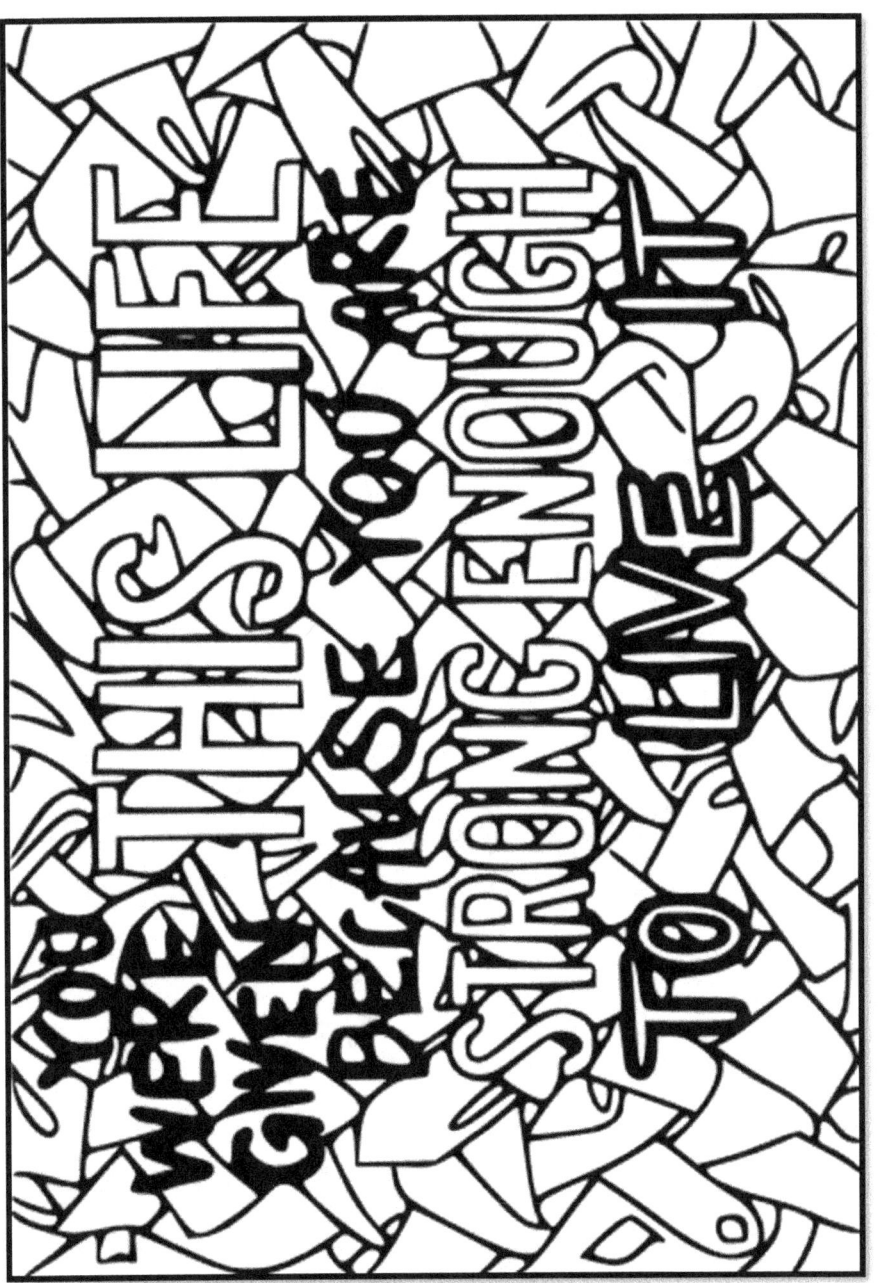

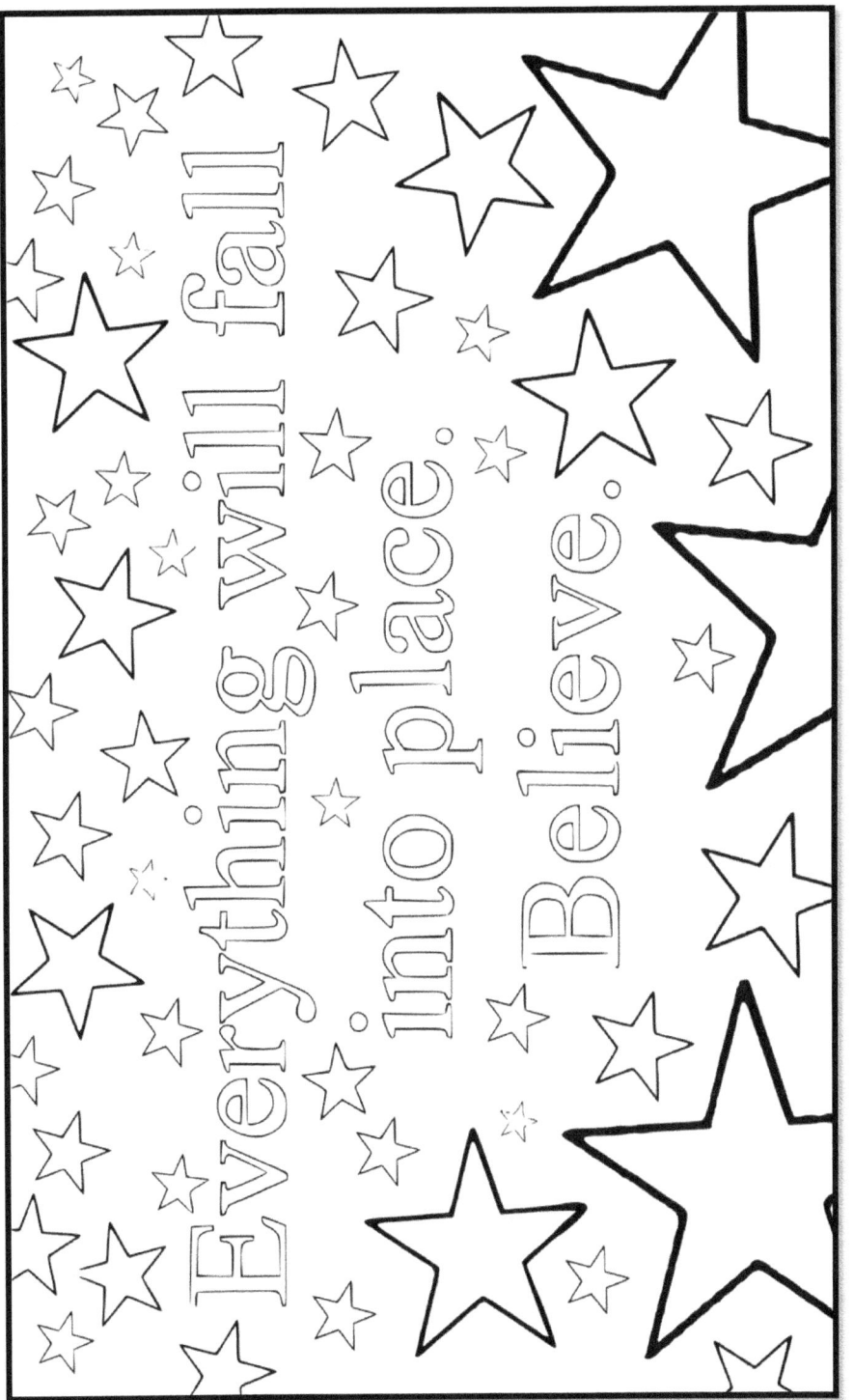

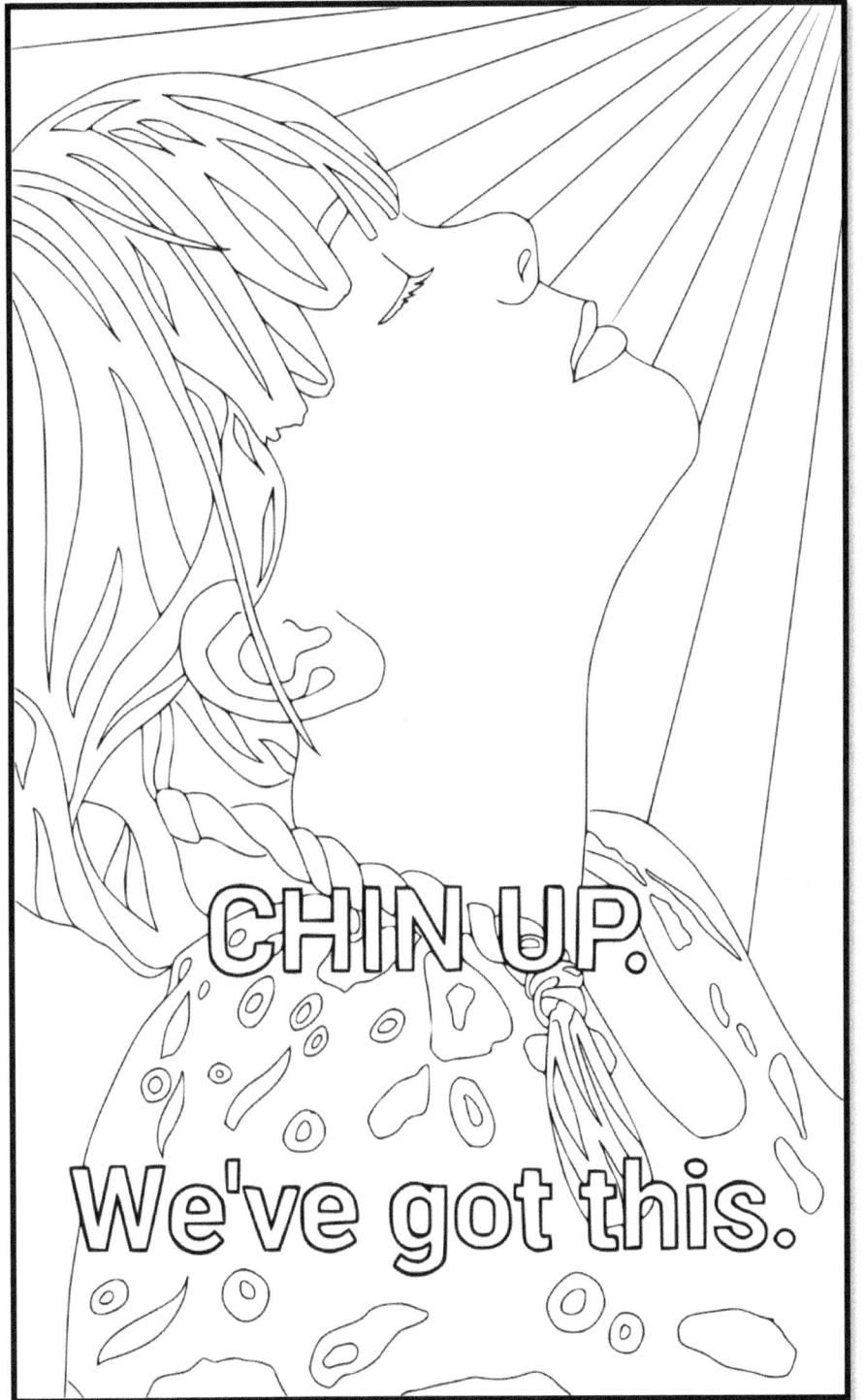

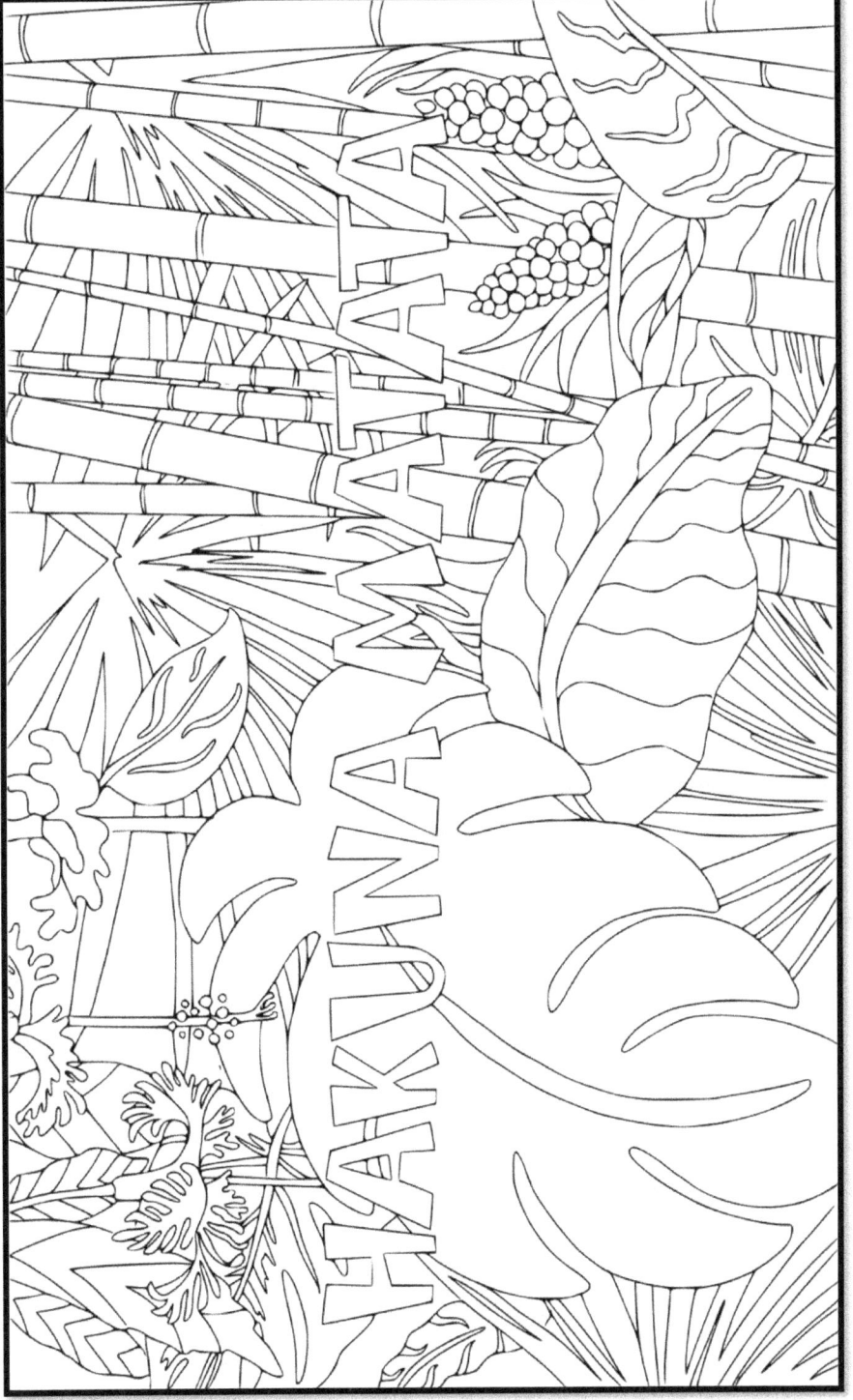

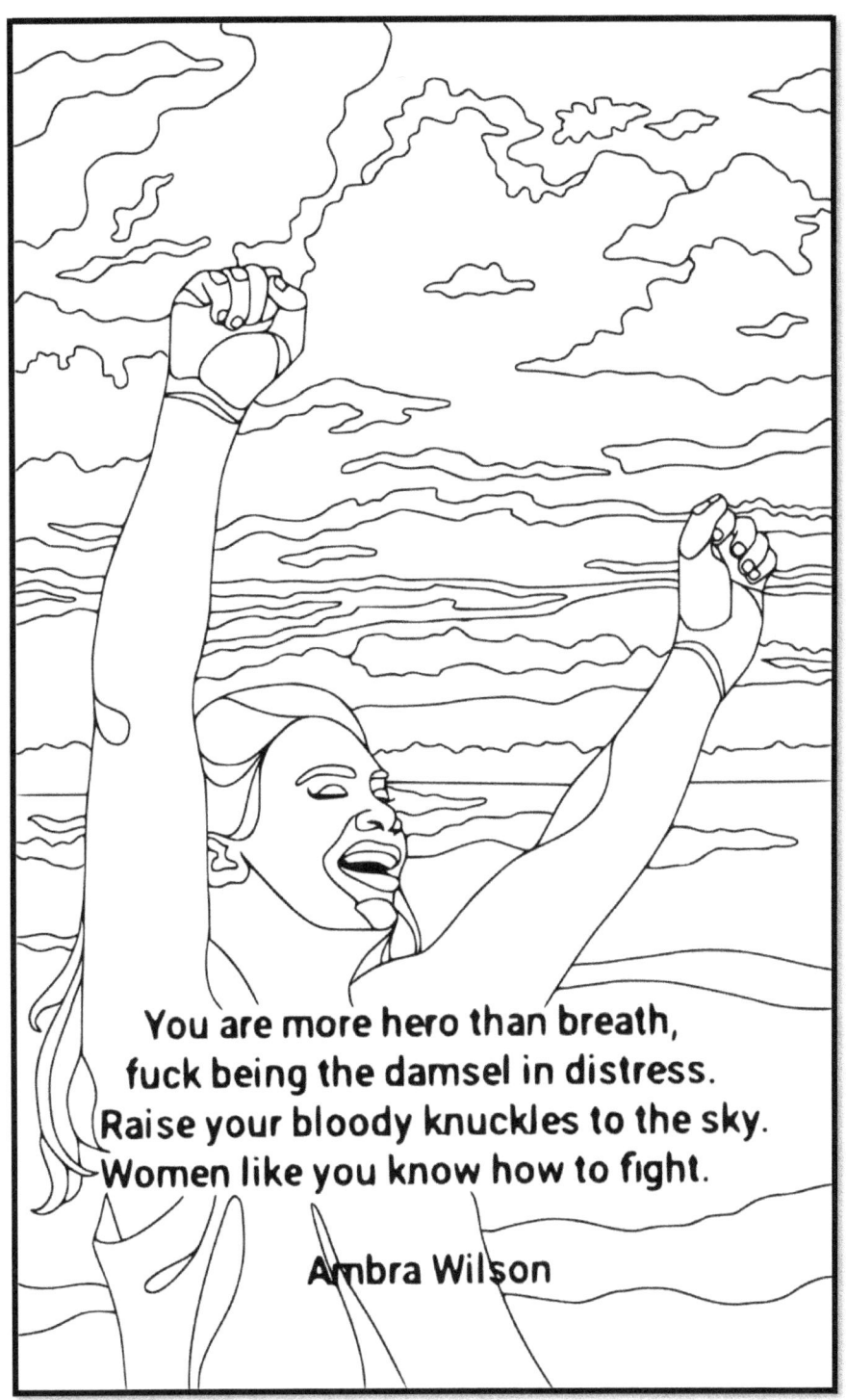

You are more hero than breath,
fuck being the damsel in distress.
Raise your bloody knuckles to the sky.
Women like you know how to fight.

Ambra Wilson

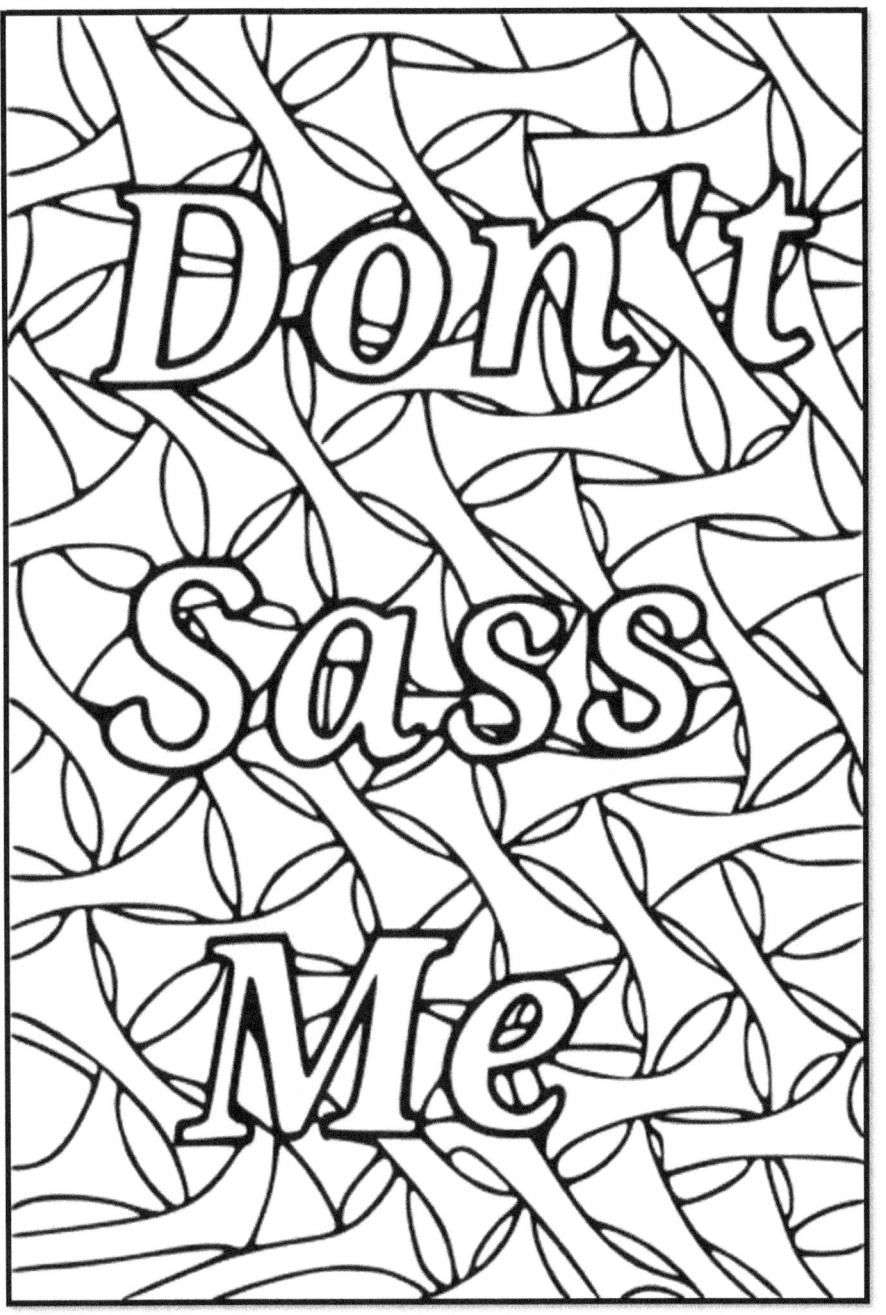

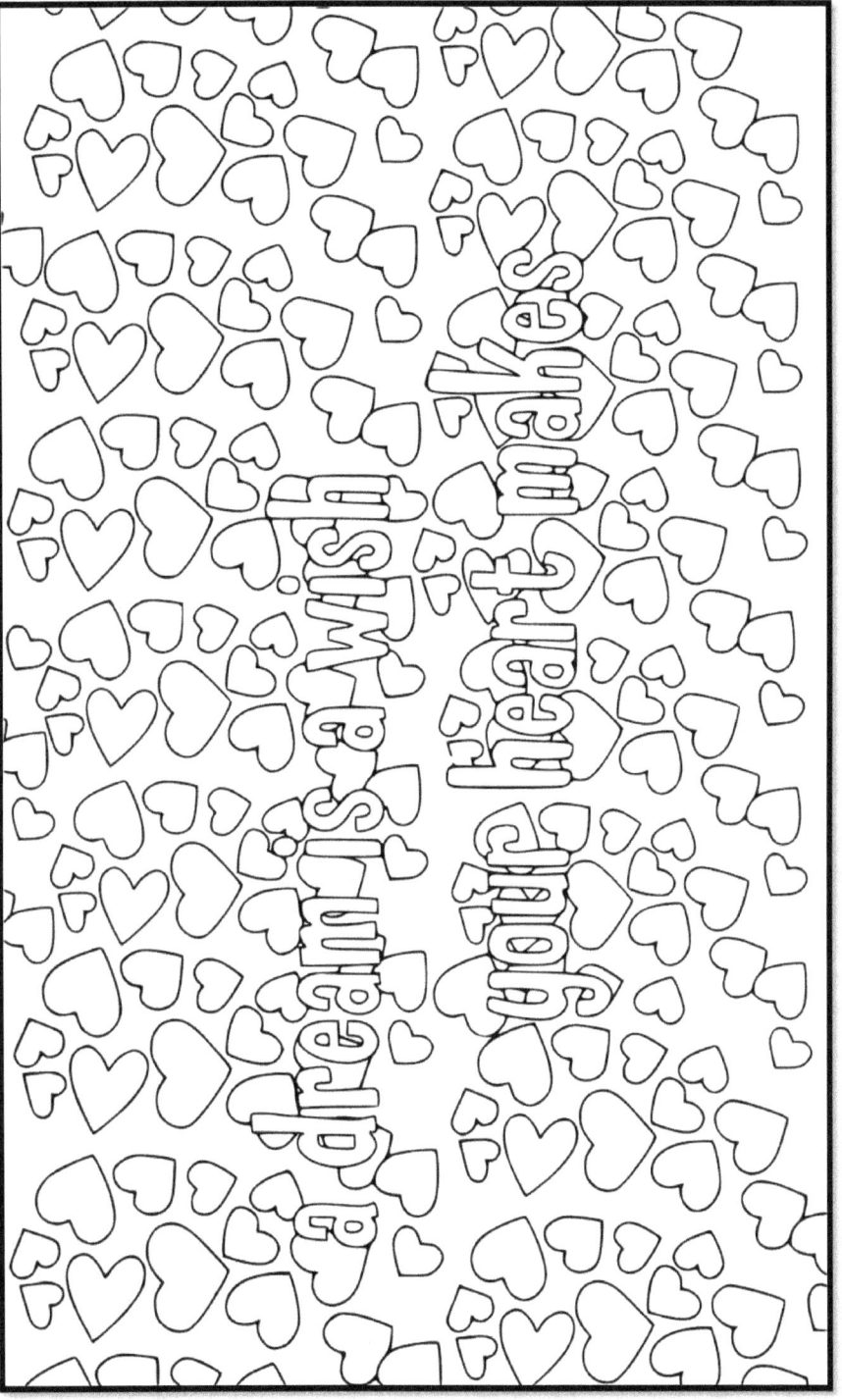

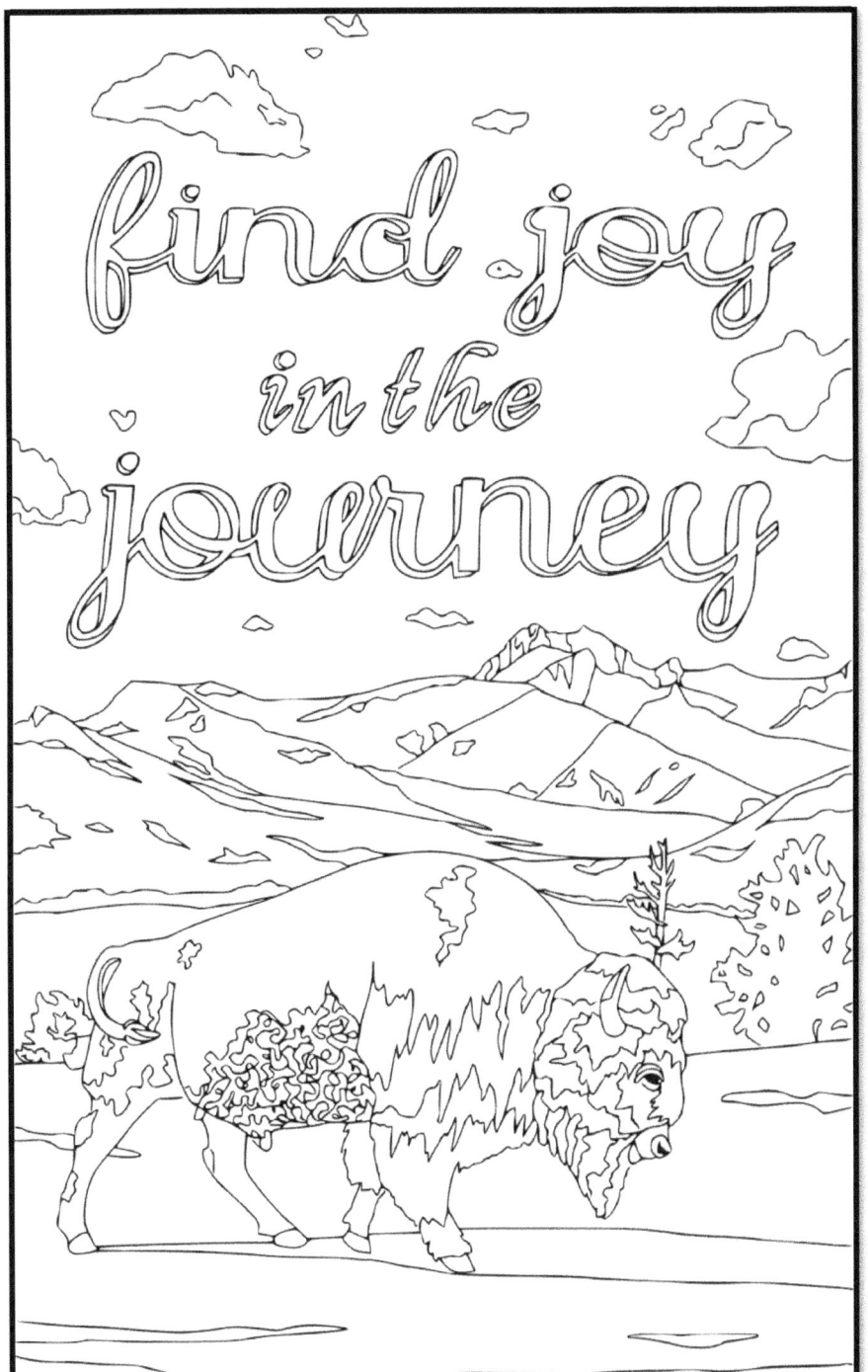

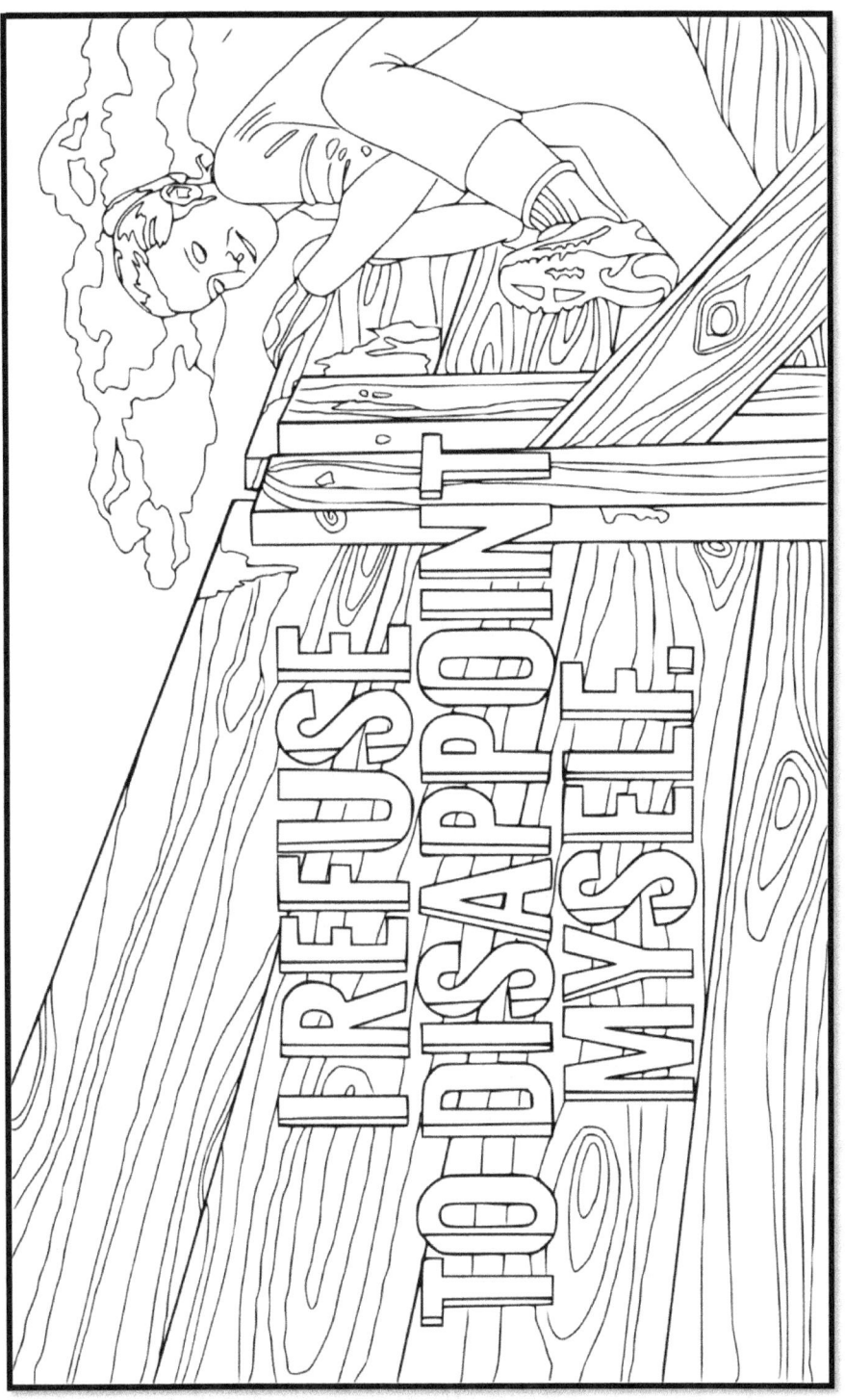

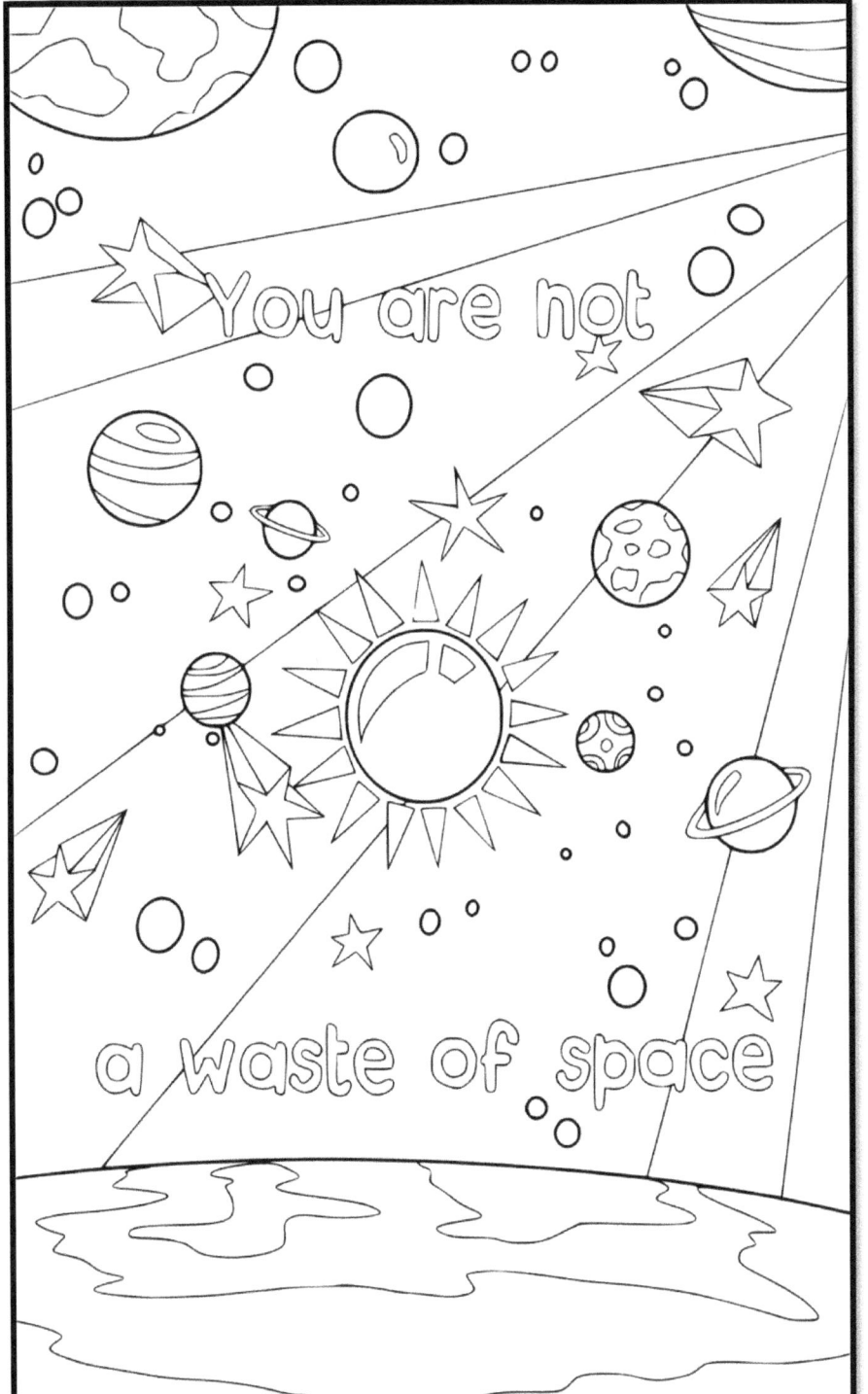

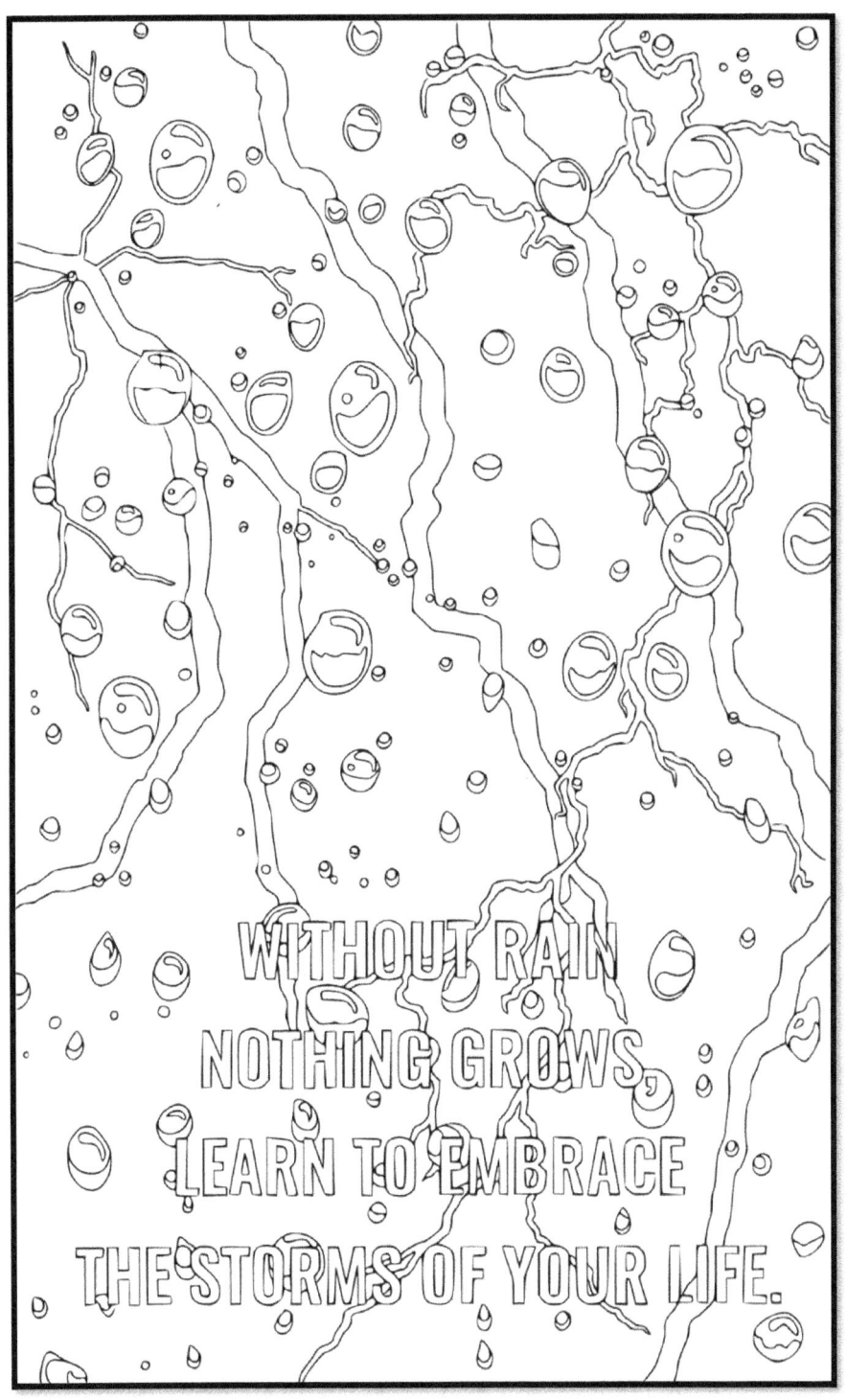

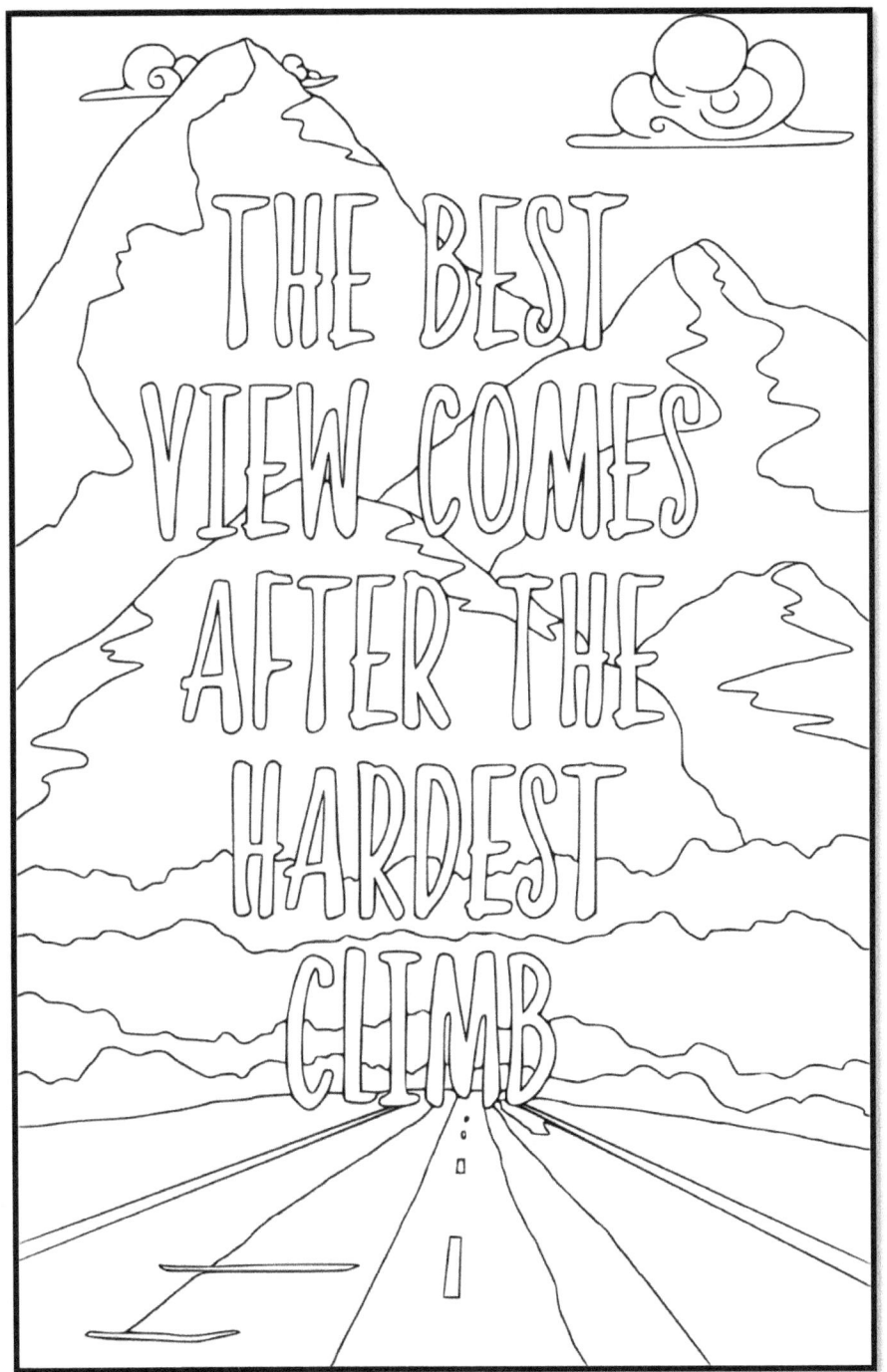

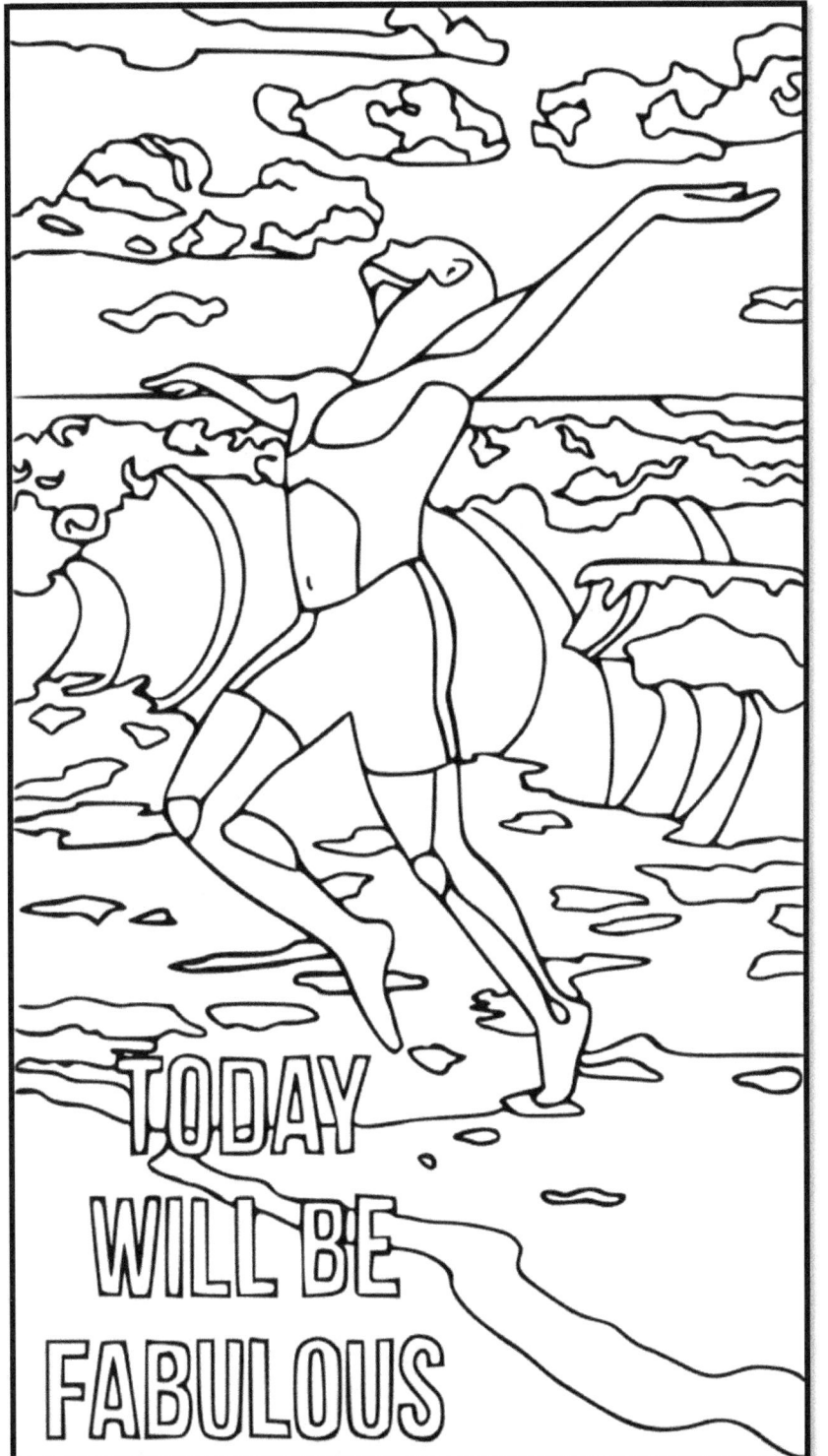

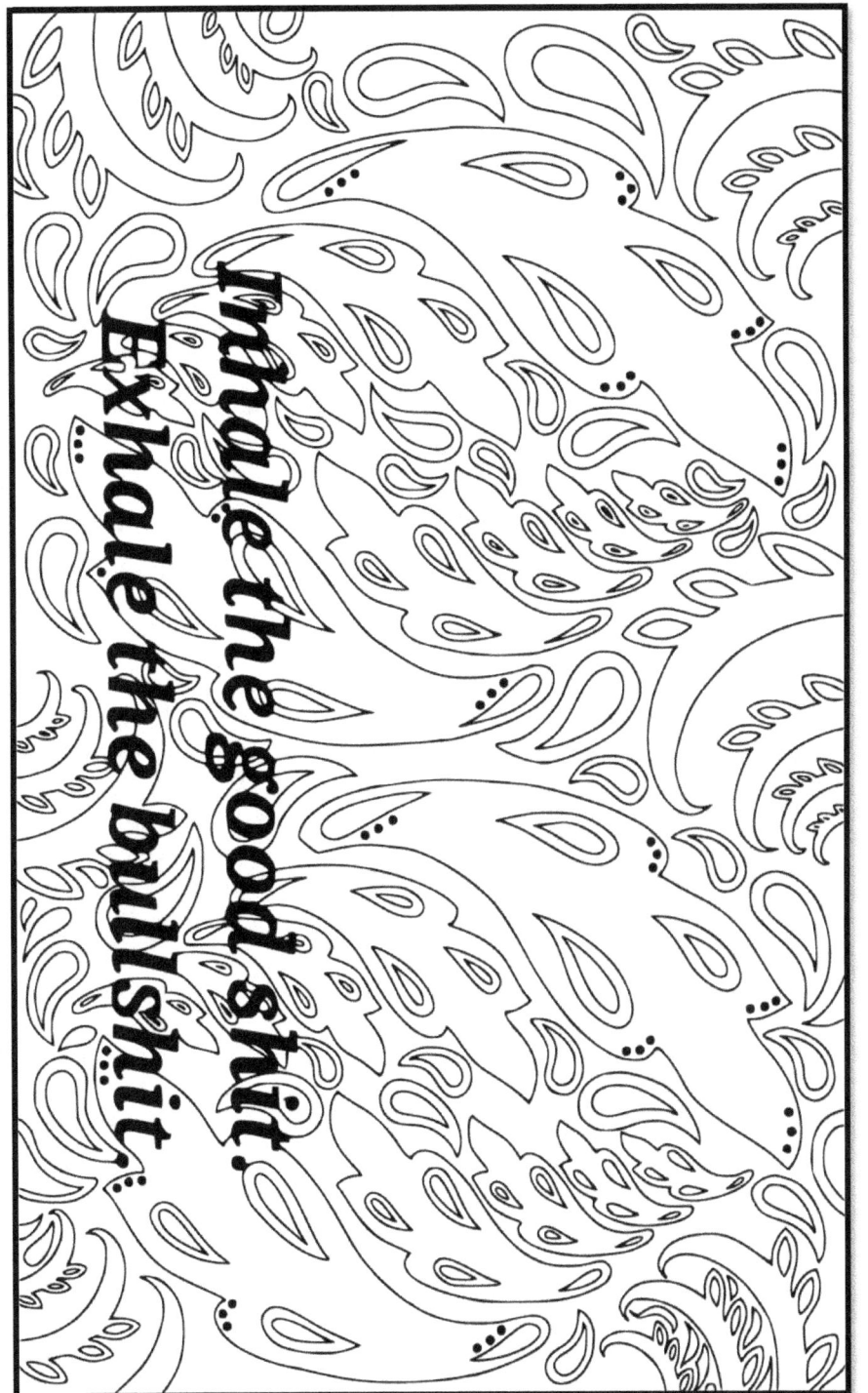

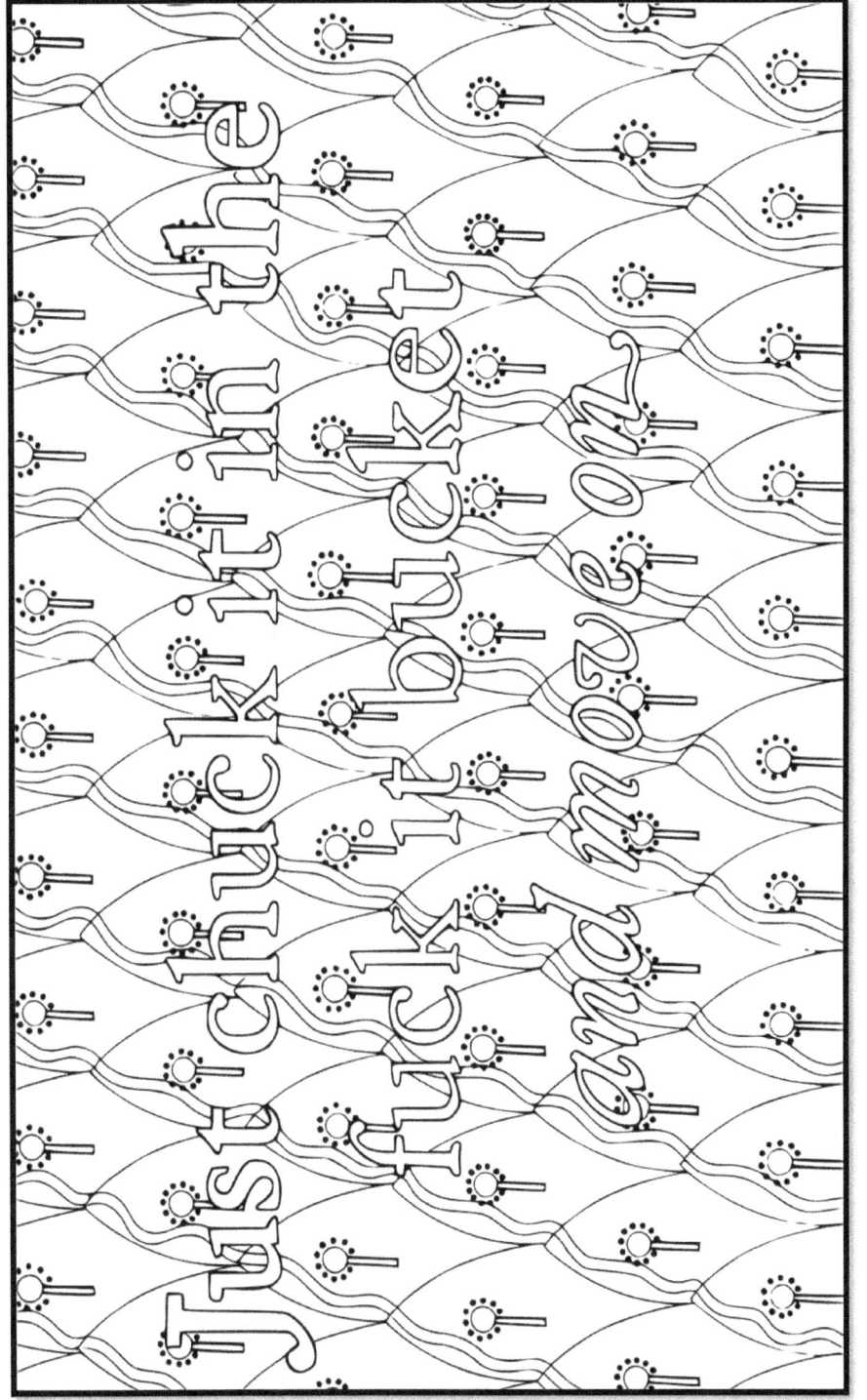

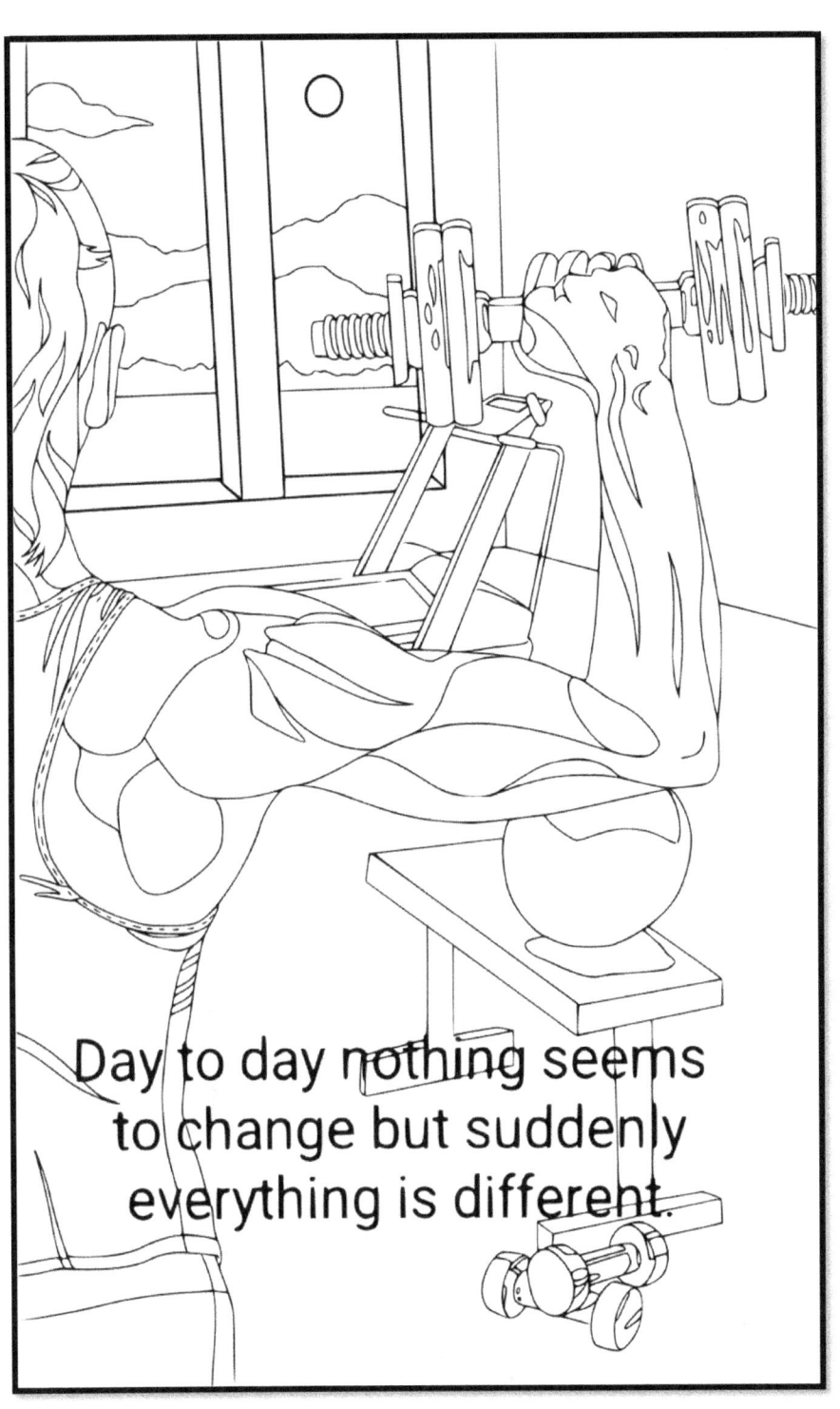

Day to day nothing seems to change but suddenly everything is different.

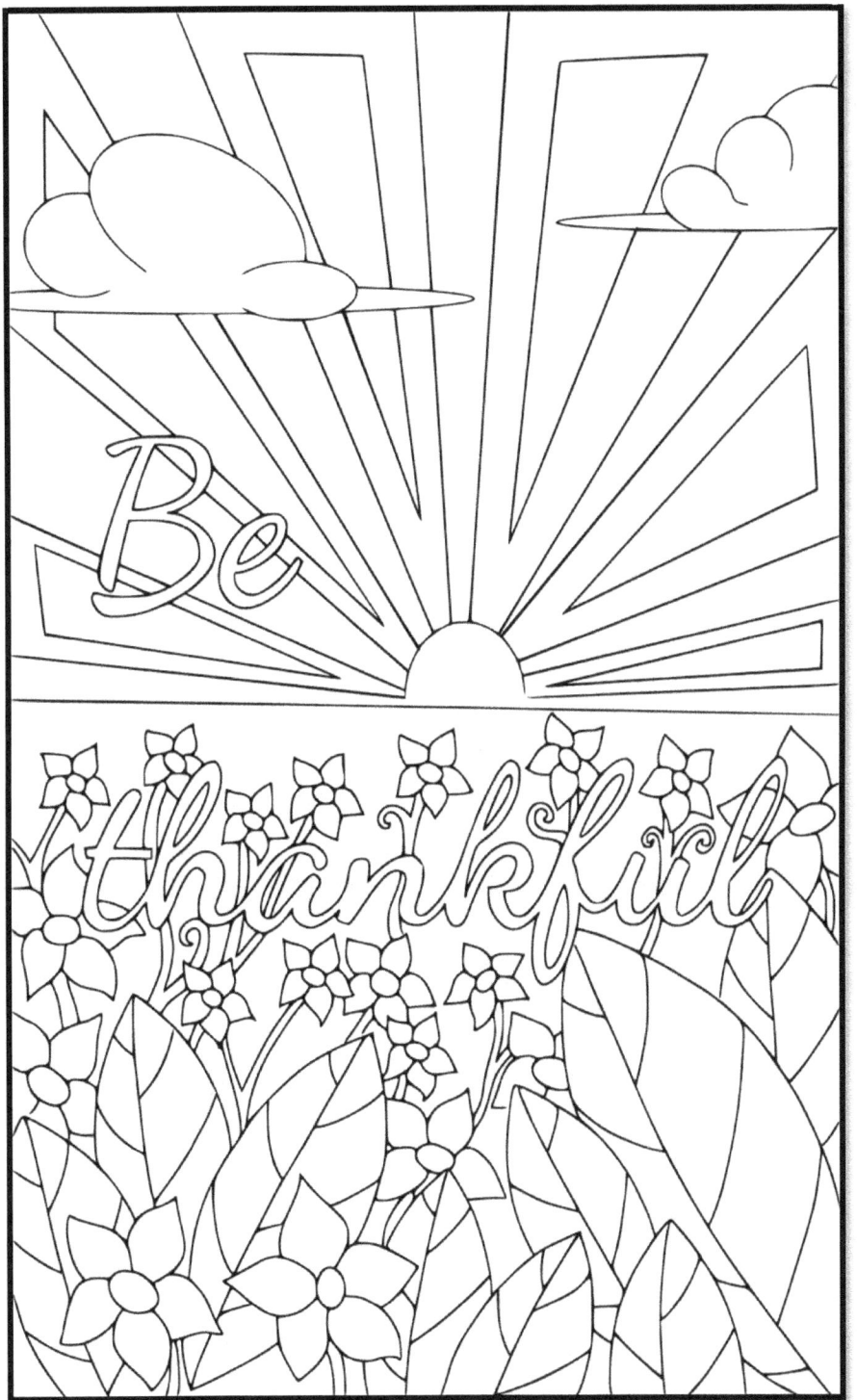

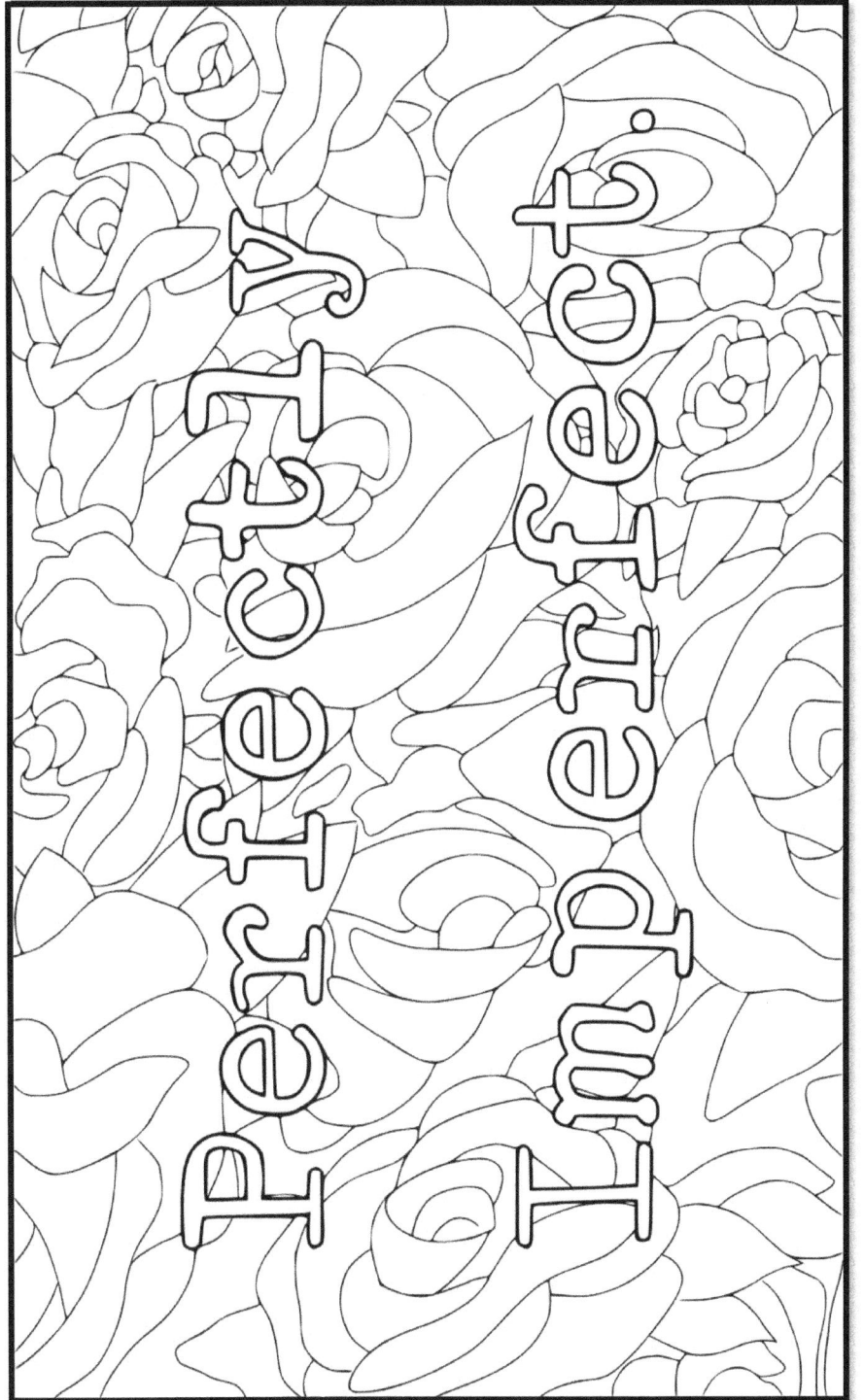

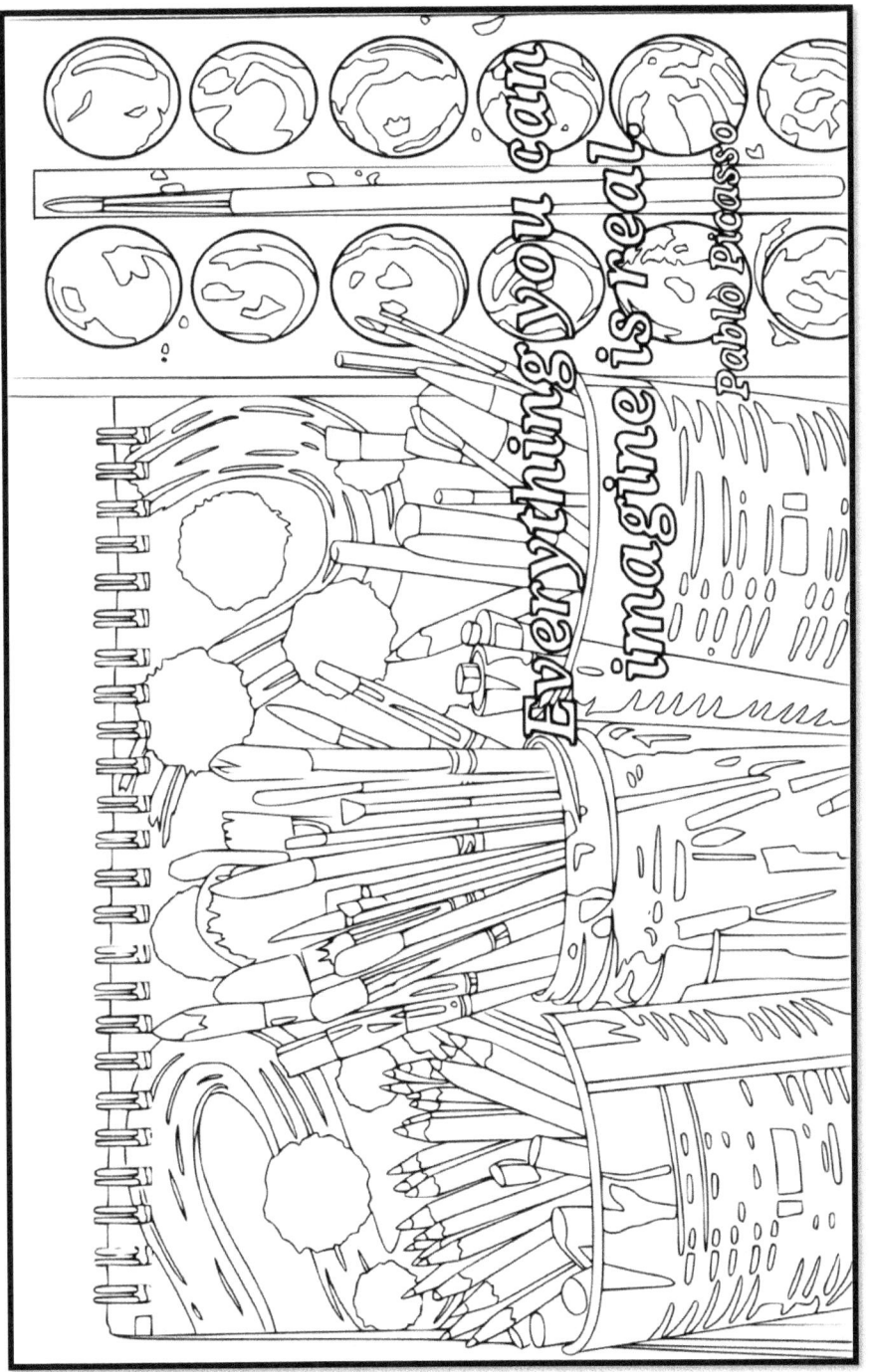

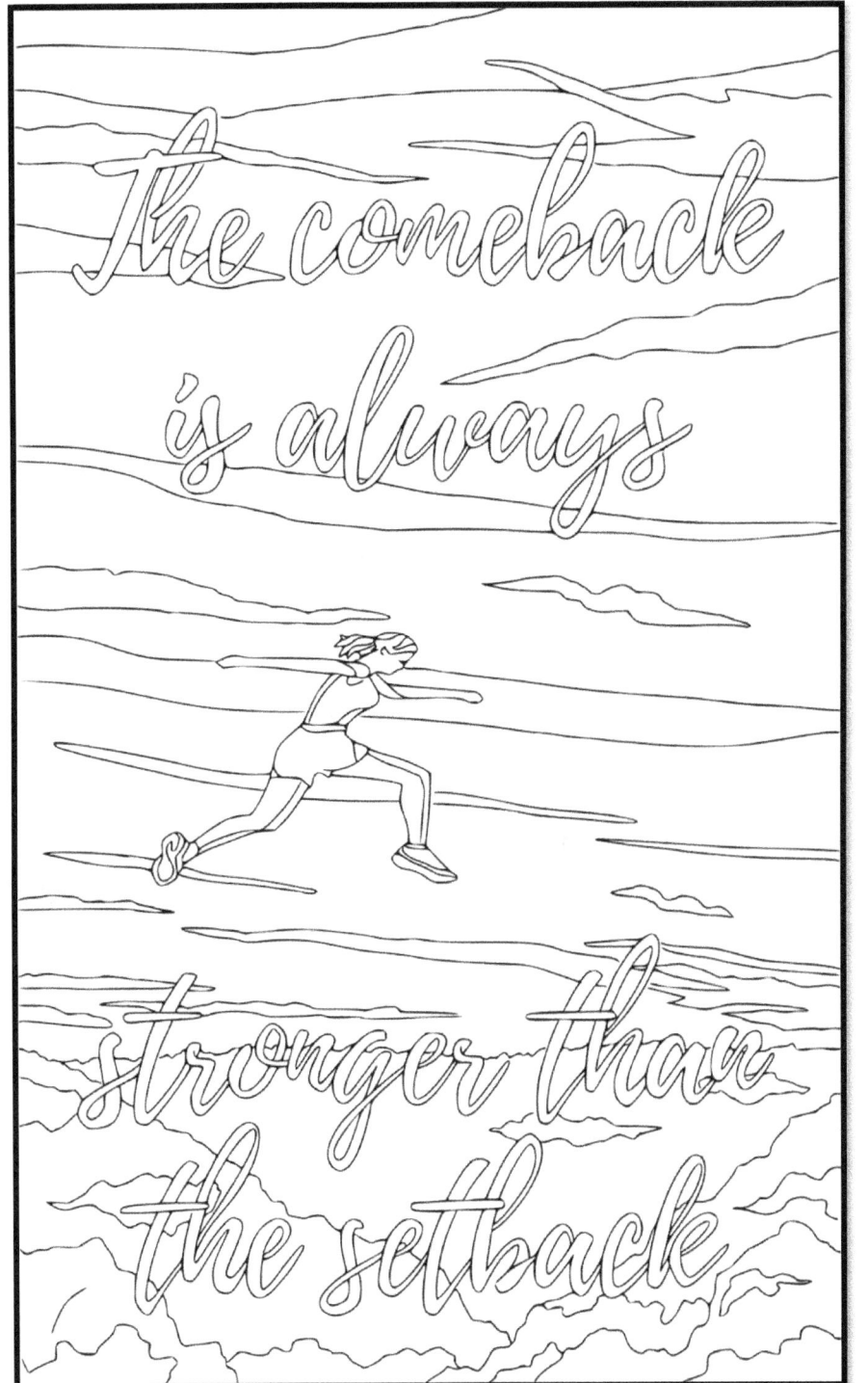

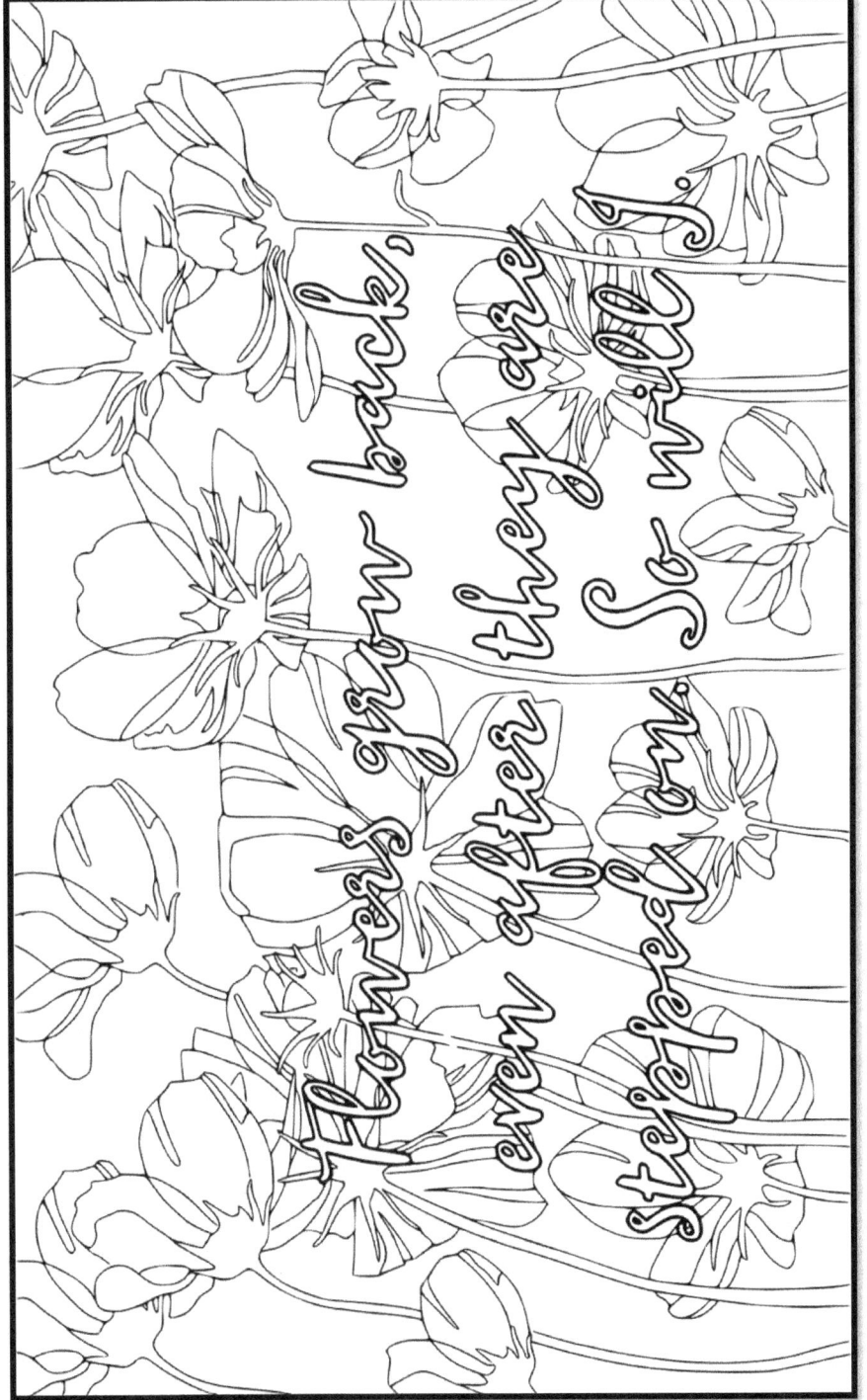

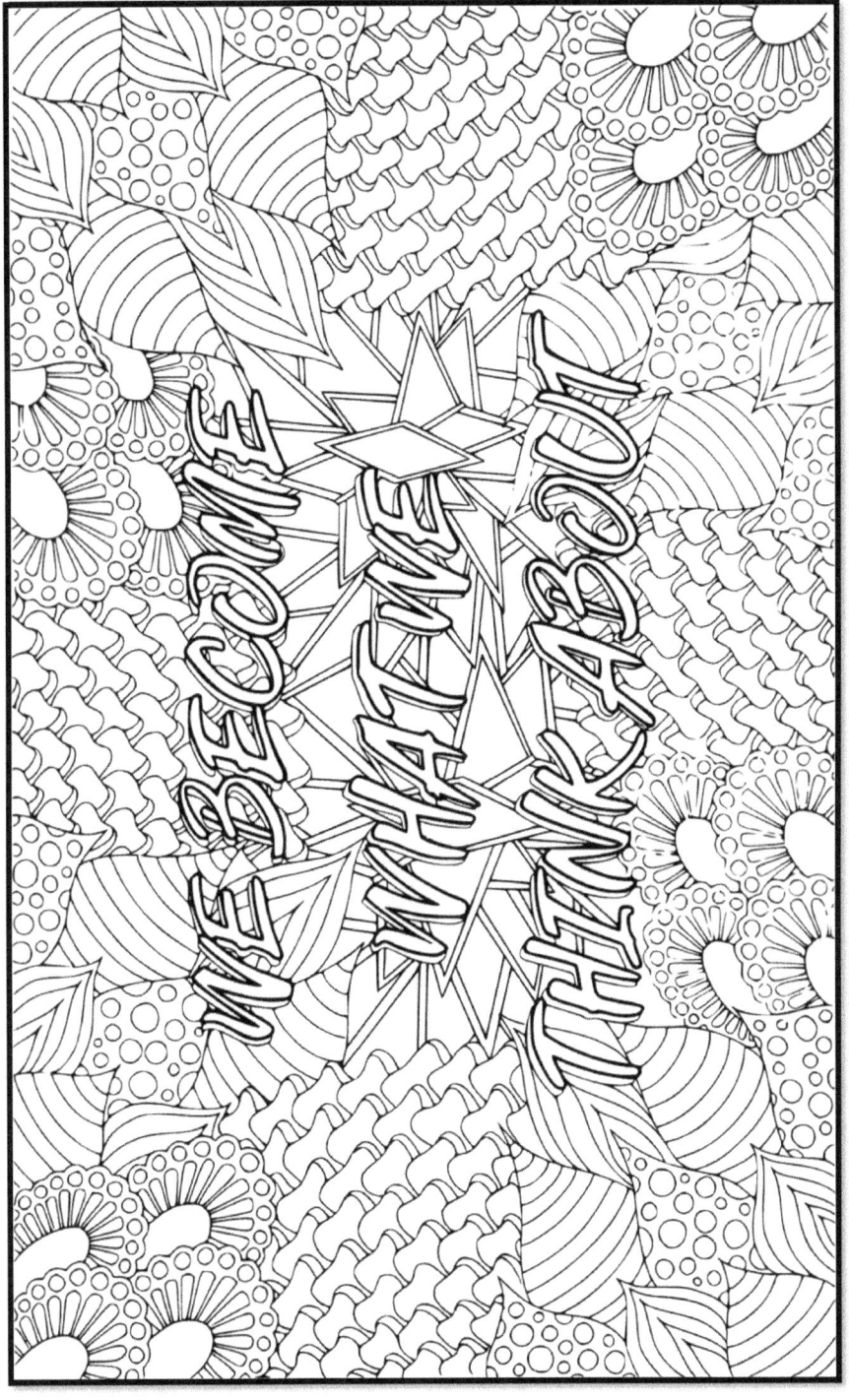

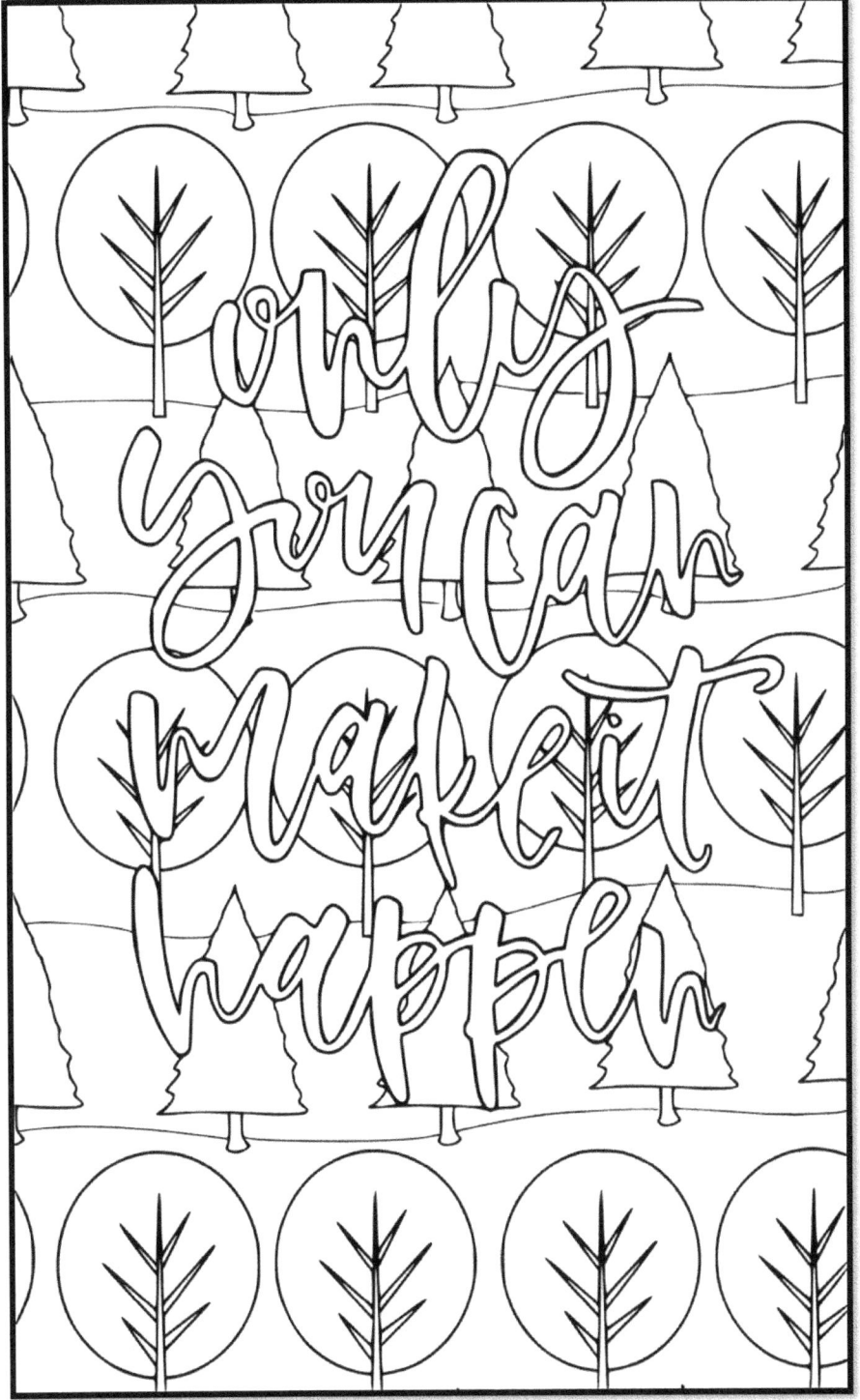

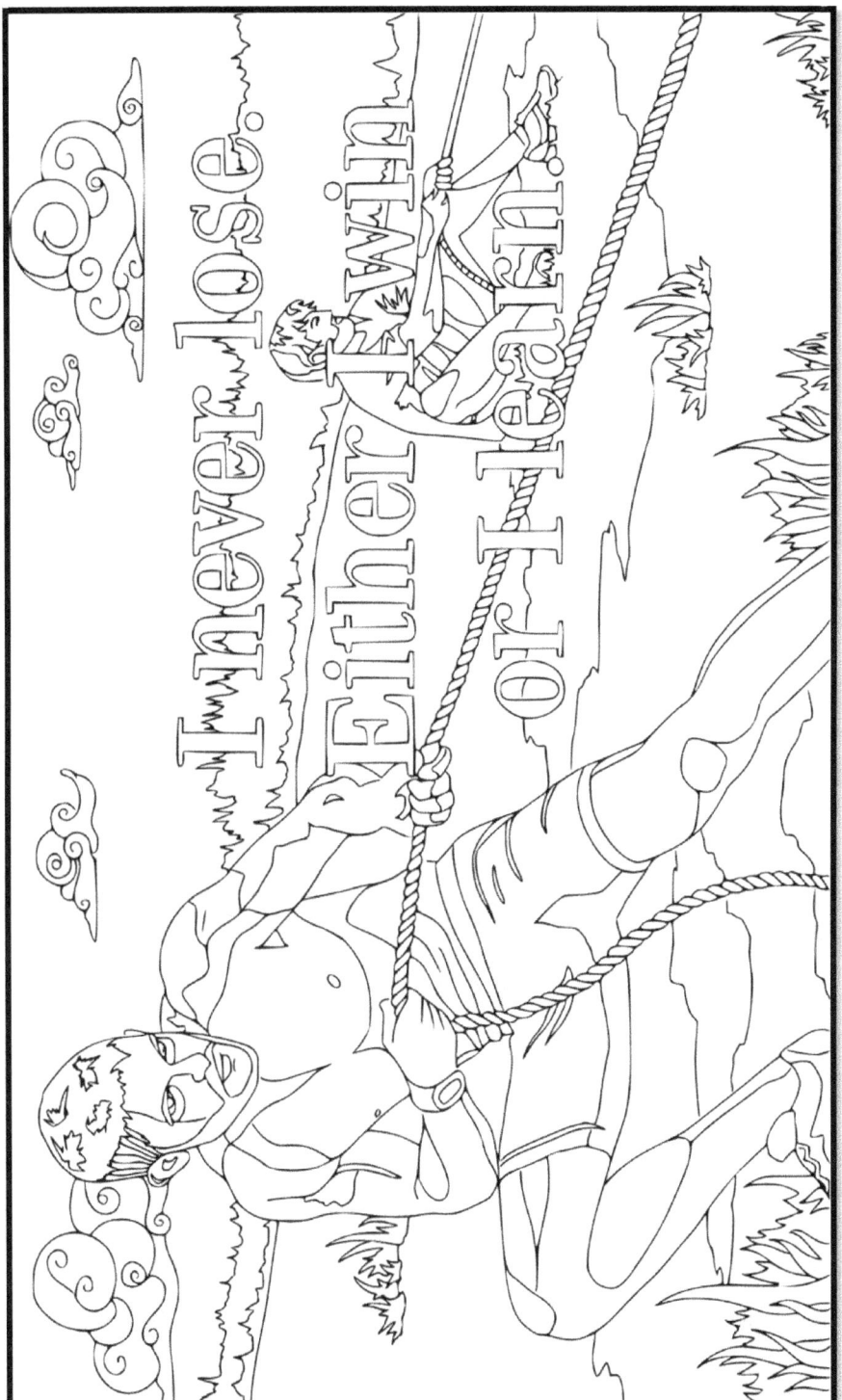

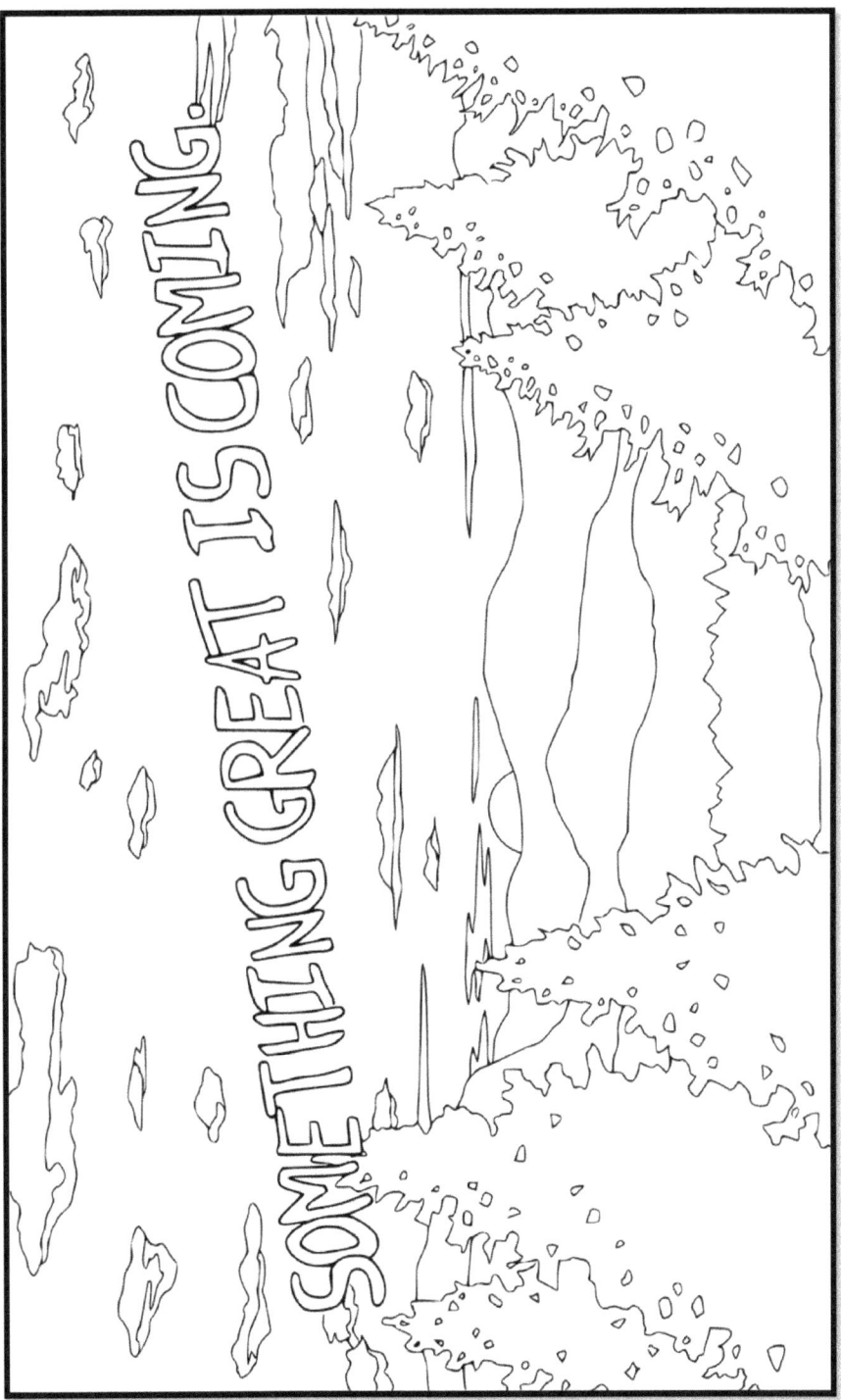

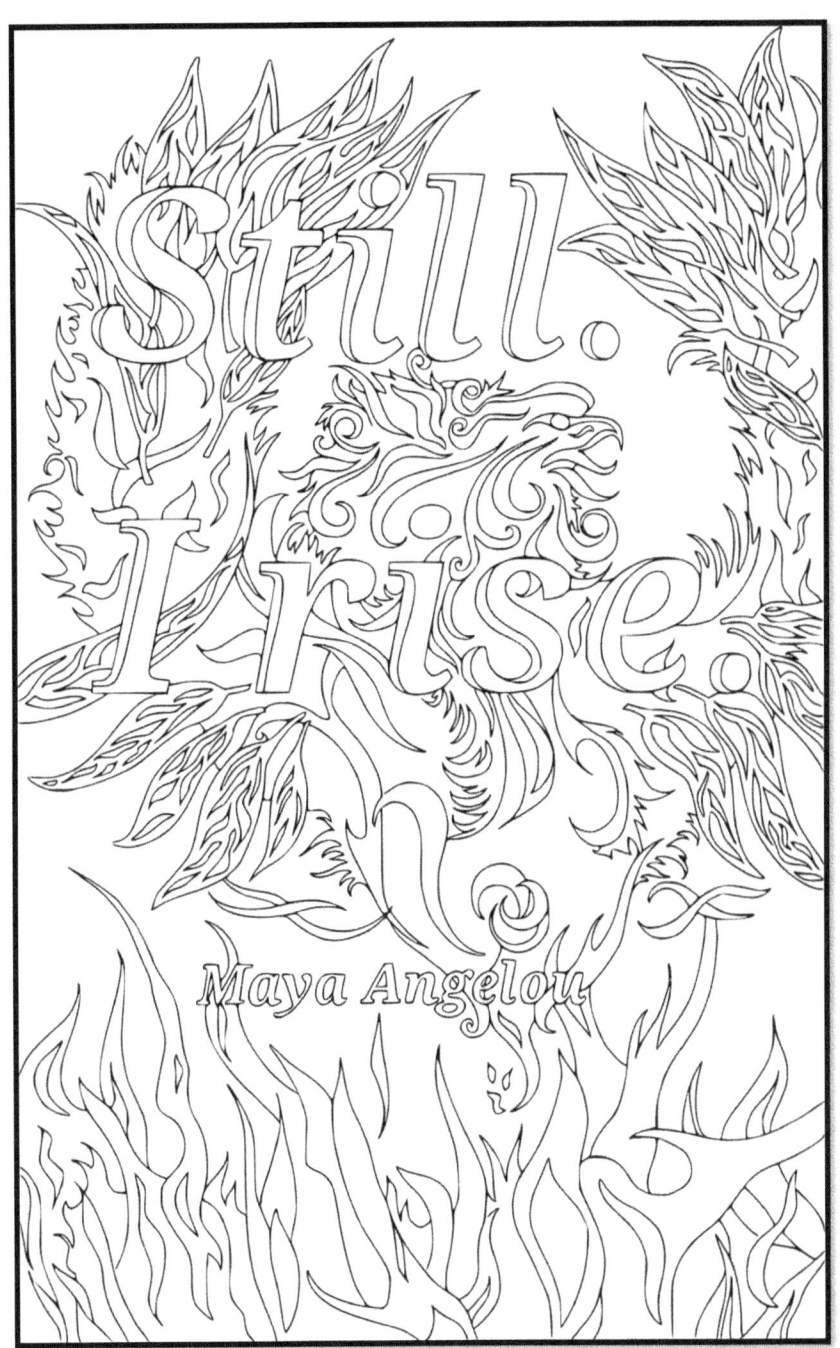

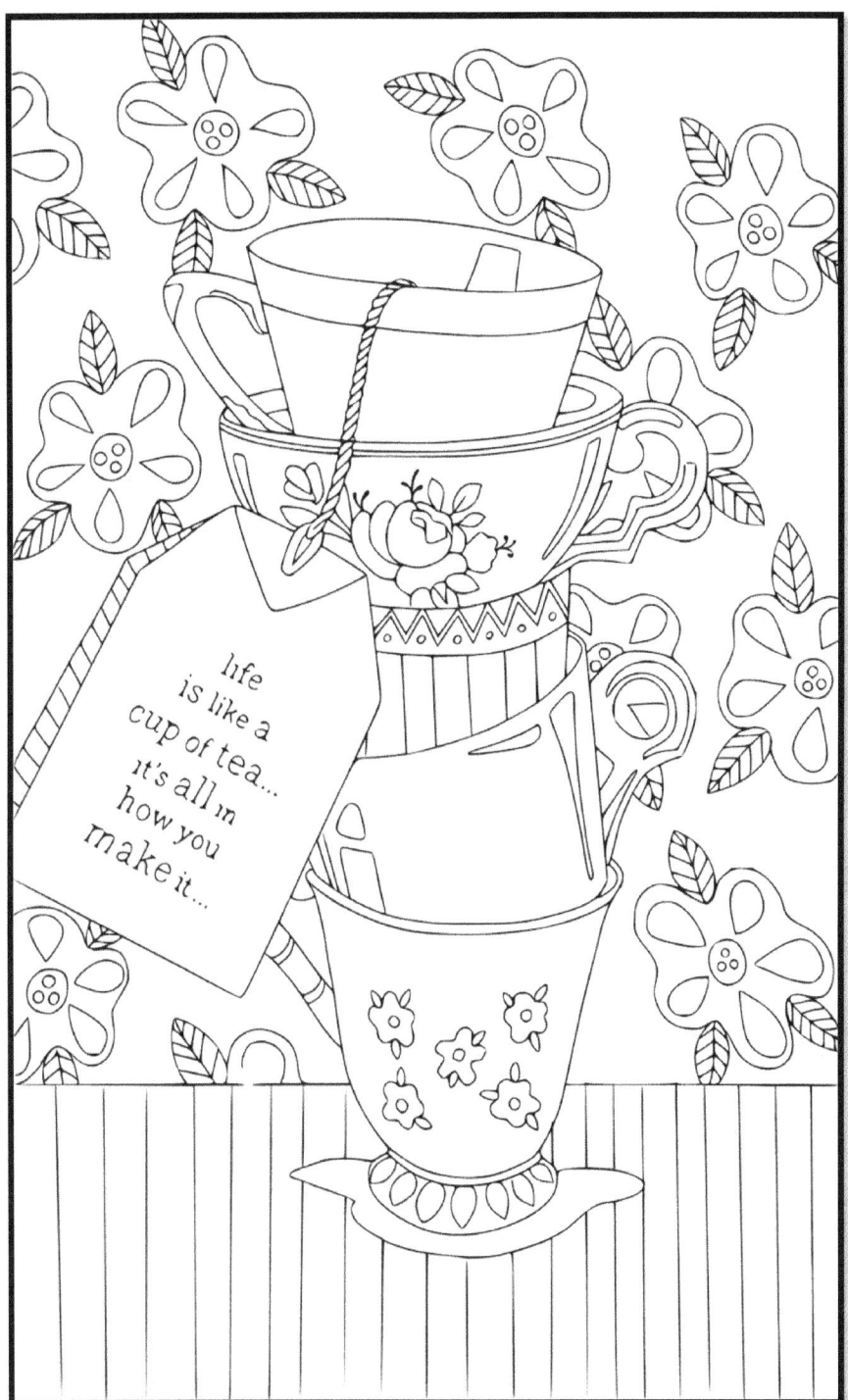

ABOUT THE ARTIST

Heather Eslinger lives near Kansas City
with her fabulously supportive husband Dean,
her crazy 13 year old twin sons and
sweet 9 year old daughter.
In addition to publishing a coloring book
Heather creates as much artwork as possible,
takes commissions,
as well as offering private art lessons.
She enjoys gardening and hiking
and spending as much time outside as possible.

For more of Heather's work
follow <u>The Roving Brush</u> on
Facebook, Instagram, Tumblr
And Twitter